주한미군지위협정(SOFA)

군민관계
임시분과위원회 1

주한미군지위협정(SOFA)

군민관계
임시분과위원회 1

| 머리말

미국은 오래전부터 우리나라 외교에 있어서 가장 긴밀하고 실질적인 우호 · 협력관계를 맺어 온 나라다. 6 · 25전쟁 정전 협정이 체결된 후 북한의 재침을 막기 위한 대책으로서 1953년 11월 한미 상호방위조약이 체결되었다. 이는 미군이 한국에 주둔하는 법적 근거였고, 그렇게 주둔하게 된 미군의 시설, 구역, 사업, 용역, 출입국, 통관과 관세, 재판권 등 포괄적인 법적 지위를 규정하는 것이 바로 주한미군지위협정(SOFA)이다. 그러나 이와 관련한 협상은 계속된 난항을 겪으며 한미 상호방위조약이 체결로부터 10년이 훌쩍 넘은 1967년이 돼서야 정식 발효에 이를 수 있었다. 그럼에도 당시 미군 범죄에 대한 한국의 재판권은 심한 제약을 받았으며, 1980년대 후반 민주화 운동과 함께 미군 범죄 문제가 사회적 이슈로 떠오르자 협정을 개정해야 한다는 목소리가 커지게 되었다. 이에 1991년 2월 주한미군지위협정 1차 개정이 진행되었고, 이후에도 여러 사건이 발생하며 2001년 4월 2차 개정이 진행되어 현재에 이르고 있다.

본 총서는 외교부에서 작성하여 최근 공개한 주한미군지위협정(SOFA) 관련 자료를 담고 있다. 1953년 한미 상호방위조약 체결 이후부터 1967년 발효가 이뤄지기까지의 자료와 더불어, 이후 한미 합동위원회을 비롯해 민 · 형사재판권, 시설, 노무, 교통 등 각 분과위원회의 회의록과 운영 자료, 한국인 고용인 문제와 관련한 자료, 기타 관련 분쟁 자료 등을 포함해 총 42권으로 구성되었다. 전체 분량은 약 2만 2천여 쪽에 이른다.

2024년 3월

한국학술정보(주)

| 일러두기

· 본 총서에 실린 자료는 2022년 4월과 2023년 4월에 각각 공개한 외교문서 4,827권, 76만 여 쪽 가운데 일부를 발췌한 것이다.

· 각 권의 제목과 순서는 공개된 원본을 최대한 반영하였으나, 주제에 따라 일부는 적절히 변경하였다.

· 원본 자료는 A4 판형에 맞게 축소하거나 원본 비율을 유지한 채 A4 페이지 안에 삽입하였다. 또한 현재 시점에선 공개되지 않아 '공란'이란 표기만 있는 페이지 역시 그대로 실었다.

· 외교부가 공개한 문서 각 권의 첫 페이지에는 '정리 보존 문서 목록'이란 이름으로 기록물 종류, 일자, 명칭, 간단한 내용 등의 정보가 수록되어 있으며, 이를 기준으로 0001번부터 번호가 매겨져 있다. 이는 삭제하지 않고 총서에 그대로 수록하였다.

· 보고서 내용에 관한 더 자세한 정보가 필요하다면, 외교부가 온라인상에 제공하는 『대한민국 외교사료요약집』 1991년과 1992년 자료를 참조할 수 있다.

| 차례

정/리/보/존/문/서/목/록

기록물종류	문서-일반공문서철	등록번호	17767 11241	등록일자	2001-06-02
분류번호	729.419	국가코드		주제	
문서철명	SOFA 한·미국 합동위원회 군민관계 임시분과위원회 - 주한미군 기지촌 정화 대책, 1971				
생산과	북미2과	생산년도	1971 - 1971	보존기간	영구
담당과(그룹)	미주	안보		서가번호	--
참조분류					
권차명					
내용목차					

마/이/크/로/필/름/사/항

촬영연도	*롤 번호	화일 번호	후레임 번호	보관함 번호
2007-9	Re-07-10	3	53	

DEPARTMENT OF THE ARMY
HEADQUARTERS 2D INFANTRY DIVISION
APO SAN FRANCISCO 96224

7 January 1971

Commissioner Min, Chung Kun
Office of the Yangju-Gun
Uijongbu, Korea

Dear Mr. Min:

The illegal activities and lack of progress in achieving required improvements in Tongduchon and the many establishments therein which depend upon the patronage of US soldiers continue to be of great concern.

At the outset, I wish to acknowledge the assistance of Yangju-Gun officials in recent months. In particular, I wish to thank Police Superintendent Ko for his sincere interest and help since his recent arrival in Uijongbu.

In my opinion, however, the police need increased support inasmuch as evidence continues to accumulate that in those areas of Tongduchon patronized by US soldiers, marijuana, barbituate pills, and other dangerous drugs are much too easy to obtain and use. Additionally, black-market activities remain high. Weapons such as switch-blade knives, straight razors and night sticks can be purchased almost at will. Sanitation is poor. Mixed (men and women) latrines are in use. Heat and ventilation in too many clubs are poor. Fire safety conditions are unsatisfactory. Venereal disease is contacted at abnormally high rates. MPC currency is readily accepted. US soldiers are given easy credit. Poor lighting and poor police of alleys and side streets creates an atmosphere conducive to crime and assaults. Too many commercial estab lishments are in areas difficult to observe and police.

Regretably, two recent attempts by Korean officials to improve conditions have not achieved significant results:

Despite the mass round-up and innoculation of business girls in Kyong-gi Province during 23-24 November 1971, the VD rate in the camp-side villages remains extremely high.

Ltr to Commissioner Min

Despite the 10-day closure on 4 December 1971 by Korean officials of two clubs in North Tongduchon (the Hong Kong Club and Blackman's Den) because of "unsanitary conditions", the clubs remain unsatisfactory not only in basic sanitation, but for other reasons as well.

A few days ago, the Hong Kong Club and Blackman's Den, both of which cater exclusively to black US soldiers in the North (black) Tongduchon area, were the subject of a formal complaint to me by a group of black U.S. soldiers. The men specified that the latrines in clubs were filthy and used by both sexes. Heat and service were poor. Girls in the clubs were loosely controlled and more likely to be infected with VD than those in South Tongduchon. They stated that drugs were a menace in North Tongduchon but alleged that they were even more prevalent and easy to obtain in South Tongduchon. These men represent soldiers -- black and white -- who believe that many local businessmen not only encourage black-white separatism, but look down upon black soldiers as trouble makers and want to keep the blacks restricted to sub-standard facilities.

Unfortunately, there remain too many in Tongduchon who encourage and advertise racial separatism and polarization. Only a few meters from the Camp Casey gates, tailor shops, clubs, music shops, and pawn shops display ethnic and racial identifiers. Much of the separatism is at the expense of black US soldiers in the form of substandard commercial facilities and sullied reputation. Much is at the expense of white US soldiers who are not safe in the North Tongduchon area.

Here again, however, I acknowledge progress. Several of the principal clubs in South Tongduchon (where 18 clubs are located in contrast to 2 in North Tongduchon) have in recent months attracted both black and white soldiers.

I am inclosing two documents for your review. One is a listing of minimum standards necessary in Tongduchon for the health, deportment, safety, basic dignity and well-being of all members of the US Armed Forces regardless of race or ethnic origin. The second is a summary of some improper activities observed in the Tongduchon areas frequented by U.S. soldiers.

It is the goal of the 2d Division to establish a joint ROK-US Committee -- at the local level -- which would inspect all commercial establishments in Tongduchon to see if they qualify for U.S. patronage. Those qualifying would be posted with a sign so indicating. Others would be off-limits.

Ltr to Commissioner Min

Such a system is now working very well in Paju-Gun. It is hoped that a level of cooperation equal to that which has been achieved in Paju-Gun can be arranged.

In order to qualify for approval for US patronage under the conditions set forth in Inclosure 1, some establishments may have to be relocated or closed. However, Tonduchon does not need an increased number of clubs. It needs to replace or to close some clubs and thus end with fewer and better clubs both on the North and South sides.

The Tongduchon situation must be viewed as a whole. I doubt that the businessmen in North Tongduchon are alone to blame for the sordid conditions which prevail in that area. If improvements in Tongduchon -- both North and South -- are not forthcoming, there is no recourse except to resort to extensive off-limits action.

The 2d Division welcomes your early suggestions.

A copy of this letter is being furnished the Commander-in-Chief, United Nations Command.

Sincerely,

2 Incl
1. Standards of Fitness
2. Improper Activities

JEFFREY G. SMITH
Major General, USA
Commanding

3

4

US COMPONENT SECRETARY MEMORANDUM

SUBJECT: Fact Finding Trips of the Ad Hoc Subcommittee on Civil-Military Relations

1. At its first meeting on 7 September 1971, the Ad Hoc Subcommittee on Civil-Military Relations outlined the purpose of its fact finding trips as follows:

> "to give Subcommittee members an opportunity to observe first - hand the situation in the local areas and to discuss and analyze with local Korean and American authorities the problems involving US military personnel in Korea and Koreans living in the vicinity of or working in US military installations."

2. Summary of trips made:

a. Total to date 29

(1) First Trip 10 Sep 71

(2) Last trip 29 Apr 75

b. Most frequently visited areas

(1) Osan Air Base/Songtan-up 5

(2) Camp Humphreys/Anjong-ni 4

(3) Camp Casey/Tongduchon 3

3. A listing of trips by date is attached at Inclosure 1.

5

FACT FINDING TRIPS
AD HOC SUBCOMMITTEE ON CIVIL MILITARY RELATIONS

29 April 75	Osan Air Base/Songtan-up Camp Humphreys/Anjong-ni
19 Dec 74	Kunsan Air Base/Kunsan City
6 Sep 74	Camp Walker, Henry, George/Taegu
23 Aug 74	Camp Page/Chunchon
18-19 Jun 74	Pusan/Chinhae
30 May 74	Hqs I Corps (ROK/US) Gp. Uijongbu
19 Oct 73	Osan Air Base/Songtan-up
8 Jun 73	Btry B, 1/2 Arty, 38th ADA Bde/Gumo
7 May 73	Osan Air Base/Songtan-up
22 Mar 73	US Army Garrison Yongsan/Itaewon
23 Feb 73	Camp Casey/Tongduchon
6 Feb 73	Osan Air Base/Songtan-up Camp Humphreys/Anjong-ni
30 Jan 73	Hqs I Corps (ROK/US) Gp/Uijongbu
9 Jun 72	USA 44th Engr Bn/Chinhae
2 Jun 72	Camp Carroll/Waegwan
10 May 72	Camp Page/Chunchon
1 May 72	ASCOM/Sinchon
30 Mar 72	Camp Casey/Tongduchon (Selected Members)
25 Feb 72	Camp Humphreys/Anjong-ni
3 Dec 71	Camp Ames/Jangdong-ni (Taejon Area)
30 Nov 71	Yongju-gol/Paju-ri/Sonyu-ri, Paju-gun (2d Div area)
14-15 Nov 71	Hialeah Compound/Pusan
28 Oct 71	US Army Garrison Yongsan/Itaewon

6

7 Oct 71	Kunsan Air Base/Kunsan City
30 Sep 71	ASCOM/Inchon
28 Sep 71	KORSCOM/Taegu
24 Sep 71	Osan Air Base/Songtan-up
13 Sep 71	Camp Humphreys/Anjong-ni
10 Sep 71	Camp Casey/Tongduchon

7

1971. 9. 24.

한 미 사 고 현 황

평 택 군

8

1. 한미 사고 발생현황

년도별	구분	계	강력	폭력	업무상과실치사상	마약	기타	비고
1970 년 총계		99	4	68	13	10	4	
7 월말 현재	70년	76	3	56	7	9	1	
	71 년	75	5	40	16	6	8	
대비		-1	+2	-16	+9	-3	+7	

2. 중요 사건 (케이 - 55 지역)

죄명	일시	장소	피해자	가해자	사건개요
살인미수	71.2.15 15:30	케이 - 55 기지정문	[redacted]	[redacted]	가해자와 피해자가 합동근무중 시비 끝에 가해자가 소지하고 있던 38구경 권총으로 피해자의 복부를 2발 발사 복부 관통상을 입고 제121 야전 병원에 입원 가료 중임.
실과	71.3.16 04:00	송탄읍 지산리 767 김영순 가	[redacted]	[redacted]	가해자는 피해자 의방안 침대에 누워 대마초(담배)를 피우다가 동 담배에 취하여 담배를 손에 진채 잠이들어 담배가 동침대에 떨어져 발화된것을 옆방에서 인지 신고하여 진화하였으나 침대 및 이불등 9,800원 상당품을 소실케 하였음.
절도	71.5.21 21:10	송탄읍 신장리 302 제일모자점	[redacted]	[redacted]	가해자는 피해자가 경영하는 점포에 동료 3 - 4명과 들어와 물건을 사려는 척이 하다가 주인이 다른 미군과 이야기 하는 사이 진열장위에 놓아둔 모자4개 시가 2,000원 상당을 절취도주

절도 날치기	71. 6.15 22=30	송탄읍 신장리 권순례가		가해자는 피해자와 71.6.14 동침한 화대3,000원을 지불하며 같이 살림할것을 요구 하였으나 이를 거절하자 피해자 손에 들고 있는 전사화대를 뺏아 갖이고 도주하자 이를 붓들려는 피해자를 주먹으로 안면 2 회 복부 3 회구타 도주함.
절도 및 장물취득	71.3.20 " 5.10 " 7.6 " 8.1	캐이55-기지 전화기 관리소 건물656호		(1) 피의자 오웬스는 통신단에 근무함을 기화로 4차에 긍하여 전화기 16 대를 절취(2) 피의자 박상오에게 2차에 걸쳐 10 대를 32,500원에 판매 하였고 (2) 피의자는 장물인 점을 충분히 인식하였음에도 (3) 피의자에게 46,900원에 판매하여 장물을 취득케 하였음.

가. 원인 및 문제점

1. 안종 평등주위에 내포된모순

2. 언어의 이해 부족으로 인한 오해

3. 관습의 차이

4. 독음으로 인한 폭력행위 (홀외에서 판매되는 독주)

5. 습관성 약품의 사용

6. 생활비 및 화대비로 인한 시비

7. 미군민의 범죄 방조 (특정외래품, 장물유출)

나. 대 책

1. 미군 당국의 자체교양 및 단속

가. 미군 자체 계획에 의거 실시중

2. 위안부 및 주민에 대한 계몽 및 단속

가. 모든 미군에 대한 친절봉사

나. 외상거래 및 군표 사용 금지

다. 담보물 및 미제 물품 취급 금지

라. 위생 관리법 검진의 철저

마. 습관성 약품의 사용금지

바. 사고 발생 및 우려시 신속한 신고

12

3. 사고 예방과 처리

가. 한미 친선 회의 운영 (월 1 회)

나. 미수사기관에 경찰관 배치

(1) 케이 - 55 기지 경찰관 4 명

(2) 케이 - 6 기지 경찰관 3 명

다. 한미 군경 합동 순찰 실시

(1) 케이 - 55 순찰대 경찰관 7 명

(2) 케이 - 6 순찰대 경찰관 7 명

라. 지서 병력보강

(1) 송탄지서 11 명

(2) 팽성지서 9 명

마. 부대주변 정화

(1) 보안사범 집중 단속

(2) 무법자 관찰

13

6. 참고 사항

가. 불매운동 사건

1. 일시

71. 4. 28 - 5. 3

2. 장소

평택군 송탄읍 신장리 및 지산리 일대

3. 피의자

미군 약 200 명

4. 피해자

신장리 지산리 업주 및 위안부.

5. 사건 개요

가. 71. 4. 28. 케이-55 기재내에서 미군 약 200 명이 모여 오산기지촌 일대의 물가가 비싸다고 가격 인하를 내세워 불매운동을 전개

나. 71. 4. 29 17:00 위안부 화대는 시간제 3 불 하루밤 6 불 기타 19 개 항목의 각종 물가를 낮추어 매긴 영문 유인물 500 매를 기지촌에 살포

다. 71. 5. 3 10:00 경 부녀회원 약 200 명이 한성홀 앞에 모여 차대 가격에 대한 유인물 산포는 인권 유린 행위라고 성토함을 경찰에서 제지 해산 시킨바 동일 15:00 전기 회원이 재차 케이-55 정문앞에 집결하여 기지 사령관에 전기 내다 선포 인권 유린 행위에 대한 사과를 요구 농성하므로 경찰에서 이를 제지 해산 시킴

나. 미 군인의 범죄방조

1. 1971. 9. 12 일 냉장고 3 개 도난 사건을 인지

14

상당여 작물 취득자 및 보관자를 검거 조사 한바 미공군 제 6314 보급지원
대 일병 [redacted] 가 절취한것이 판명됨,

2, 1971, 9, 18 00:08 평택군 송탄읍 송탄지서 앞에
세워 [illegible] 경기영 7-3892 호를 미제 6988 보안부대 중사 [redacted]
[redacted] 당 30 년이 절취 도주 하였다는 신고
에 의거 평택 경찰서 진위 지서에서 차량 검문 검거함,

15

10-4-71

상관보고

한.미 군민관계 임시분과위원회의 현지 답사

1. 한.미 군민관계 위원회는 미 2사단 지역인 동두천 (9. 10)과 미 제 23지원단이 있는 평택 (9. 13)의 현지답사에 이어 다음과같은 현지 답사를 하였음.

가. 일시및 장소 :

9. 24. (금)	평택군 송탄읍 사무소 미 제 314 항공사단 사령부 (오산 항공기지)
9. 28. (화)	대구시청 미 후방지원사령부, 제 19 지원단 사령부 (대구 캠프 "헨리, 워커")
9. 30. (목)	인천시청 미 제 20 지원단 사령부 (ASCOM) 기지주변 시찰

16

나. 참 가 자 :

한국측

외무부	북미 2과 서기관	김 기 조
〃	〃 사무관	권 찬
내무부	지방국 관리과장	백 세 현
〃	치안국 외사과 3.총경	이 병 호
법무부	송무과 검 사	정 구 영
〃	검찰과 검 사	현 홍 주
보사부	보건관리관	민 창 동
교통부	관광국 진흥과장	김 접 영

미국측

Capt. Frank M. Romanick	Assistant Chief of Staff, J5 US Forces, Korea
Mr. Robert A. Kinney	Chief, International Relations Branch, J5 Division US Forces, Korea
Col. David P. Heekin	Deputy Chief of Staff Eighth US Army
Col. Robert G. Eklund	Vice Commander, 314th Air Division, Air Forces, Korea

17

Col. Bruce T. Coggins	Staff Judge Advocate US Forces, Korea/ Eighth US Army
Col. James K. Pope	Surgeon US Forces, Korea/ Eighth US Army
Col. Robert J. Kriwanek	Provost Marshal Eighth US Army
Mr. John P. Leonard	Political Section American Embassy

2. 시찰 주요 내용

가. 오산 기지

일차적으로 사건경위에 관한 한국측 "브리핑" 을 청취하였는 바, 참석자는 평택군수, 경찰서장, 송탄읍장, 관광협회장, 부녀협회장및 주민대표들 이었음.

가장 특기할 사항은 K-55 기지 병사들의 "불매운동사건" 임. 즉, 71.4.28. - 5.3. 미군기지 병사 약 200명이 기지촌 일대에서 소비자 물가가 비싸다는 이유로 불매운동을 이르켰고 뿐만 아니라, 위안부 화대를 $6에서 $3로 내리자는 데모를 전개하고 영문 유인물 500여매를 기지촌에 살포 하였음. 기지촌 부녀회원들은 화대가격에 대한 공개적인 시위(비)와 유인물 살포는 인권 유린행위라고

18

크게 반발하였으나 경찰의 중재로 원만히 해결되었음.

미측 "브리핑" 사항은 현재 흑백및 한국인 주민과의 충돌사건이 다소 빈번하나 EOT (Equal Opportunity Treatment)대원의 활약으로 원만한 관계를 유지하고 있음.

나. 대구 기지

대구 시청의 "브리핑" 에서는 부시장, 남대구 경찰서장, 칠곡군수, 관광협회장및 주민대표 다수가 참석하였으며, 특기사항은 미군들의 수준이 주민들의 수준보다 월등히 낮아 사소한 충돌사건이 빈번하나 현지 지방관서장과 미군 기지 사령관과의 정기적인 한.미 친선회의의 개최로 원만한 해결을 보고 있음.

미측 "브리핑" 중 특기사항은 흑인 군인들이 그들의 "전용 클럽" 을 선정하고 (This is our territory 라 주장한다고 함) 백인들의 출입을 금지시킬뿐만 아니라 그 주변 일대 클럽에도 백인들의 접근을 위협하고 있어, 영업에 큰 지장을 초래하고 있음.

다. 인천, 부평 기지

한국측 에서는 부시장, 부평 경찰서장, 부평 동장 등이 참석했으며, 타지역과 비교해서 특기할만한 사실은

19

마약, 특히 대마초 (marijuana)의 사용자가 많다는 점임. 집중적인 마약단속을 위해 한.미관계 책임자들의 공동노력이 요청되고 있음.

20

한. 미 군,민관계 임시 분과위원회

현 지 답 사 보 고

〔1971. 10〕

1. 동두천 (1971. 9. 10)

가. 한.미인 간 충돌문제

(1) 한국업자측은 누구나 모두 고객이므로 차별대우를 할 이유가 없으나 흑인을 접대한 업태부를 백인이 상종하지 않으므로써 생기는 자연발생적 결과이며, 일부 클럽에 백인이 못오도록 흑인들이 행패하기 때문에 생기는 결과라고 보고있음.

(2) 미국측은 "홍콩", "부랙크 덴" 클럽과같이 흑백 차별이 한국인들의 initiative 로 발생한 것이며, 따라서 이러한 차별을 일삼는 클럽에는 off-limits 를 내릴수 밖에없다고 주장함.

(3) 미군 당국은 백인군인에 대한 교육이 필요하며, 흑인 극단분자들의 통계로서 소위 흑인클럽 sector 를 없앨것이 요청됨. 한국 업태부와 업자들에 대한 계몽도 필요함.

금족령을 내리기에 앞서 사전통고와 시정 유예기간을 주어야 할 것이며, 이런 문제의 해결을 위하여 한.미 친선협회를 통한 상호협의가 절실히 요청됨.

21

(4) 고객대접상 차별의 명확한 한계의 설정이 필요한바, 관광업소 출입제한과 식음료 구별판매의 경우에는 차별이 될수 있으나 "위안부의 고객선택"의 자유는 제외되어야 한다.

나. 한.미인 관련 범법사건

(1) 음주, 치경, 과실, 흑백, 마약등의 사건이 증가추세를 보였는바, 이러한 사건들이 발생하는 원인은 :

(가) 미2사단은 철수한 미 7사간보다 친결도가 낮으며 현지 주민들과 친분관계를 향상시키려는 노력이 없다.

(나) 언어의 장벽과 욕설이 성행하며, 미군인의 행패가 심하다.

(다) 주민간에 미군의 추가 감축에 대한 기우가 있으며, 금족령으로 인한 업자들의 원성과 경제적 피해가 극심하다.

(라) 미 헌병이 한국인 주거지에 침입, 가택수색을 하는 사례가있고 한국인을 영내로 동행하여 심문하는 사례가 있는바, 이에 주민들은 반감을 갖고있다.

(마) 미군인 사복착용 외출로 품위를 유지 못한다.

22

(2) 이러한 사건의 방지를 위하여 한.미 합동순찰, 미군인에 대한 지도 계몽, 위안부 자치회의 활동 강화, 업자와의 협조, 유관기관간의 협조등이 필요함. 그리고 미측에 대한 요망사항으로서 :

(가) 외출 미군인의 단속 (군복착용, 폭행단정등)및 출입처 제한 (정부허가 관광 유양업체에만 출입을 국한시킨다)

(나) 한국인에 대한 조사, 연행, 민가 수색등 금지

(다) APO 에 의한 마약류의 밀수 방지 (한.미 협동 조치)

(마) 외출 미군의 휴대품 반출을 극도로 제한

(3) 특히 인구 7만 이상인 동두천에 경관이 22명뿐인바, 이의 대폭 증강과 부패 경관의 숙정이 요망됨.

다. 보건 위생

동두천 지역에는 약 1,600명의 위안부중 1,000여명만이 관광업소에 등록하고 있으며 성병 검진과 진료가 불철저한 것으로 보이는바, 형식을 벗어나 그 철저를 기하기 위하여 보건소 (현재 의사 4명)의 증강과 여성들에 대한 효율적인 계몽 등이 요청되며, 대마초등 환각제의 구매가 가능한 이지역에서 철저한 마약 단속반의 상치 내지 증원과 한.미 합동활동(경찰과

23

협조하여)과 동시에 미군인의 허가된 출입처외의 출입 제한이 긴급히 요청됨.

라. 동두천의 인구는 7만 이상인바, 아직도 읍사무소 밖에 없으며, 군청이 멀리떨어진 의정부에있어, 행정사무에 지장이 많음. 조속히 시로 승격시켜 증강된 관계관서가 설치되어 지방행정에 임하여야 함.

마. 현지 한.미 친선협회 조직 운영

미 7사단 주둔당시 한.미 친선협회가 (한국측 군수, 서장, 협회장등, 미측 사단장, 각 참모등) 있어 월 1회 교대로 모여 문제점을 논의하여 한.미 협조리에 처리하였으나, 현재는 사단장의 반대로 없어졌음. 이러한 협회의 부활이 필요함. 현재는 민사참모와의 개별적 접촉만이 있을뿐임.

2. 평 택 (1971. 9. 13)

가. 한.미인 간 충돌사건

과거 고객과의 문제점은 원인면에서 동두천과 유사하나 71. 9.의 사건은 흑인들이 업소에서 업태부에게 행패및 인권유린을 하여 시작된 것인바, 양측의 공동노력으로 개선의 징조를 보이고 있음.

오산의 경우 업태부에 대한 Club pass 라는 형식으로 신분조사를 하고 있는바, 그의 폐지가 요망됨.

24

또한 안정리 6개 클럽에 대하여 진입로 협소 (2.5 - 3m) 로 흑백사고의 원인이 된다는 이유로 내린 금족령은 사유가 부당하며, 시정이 불가능한 요청이므로 다른 방편이 마련되어야 할 것임.

흑백 병사에 대한 훈계와 업자및 업태부에 대한 계몽이 계속 필요하며, 한.미 친선협회를 통한 협의로 개선에 노력 하여야 할 것임.

나. 마약 단속

평택지역의 마약문제는 동두천과같이 심한것이 아니며, 소수의 대마초, 환각제 사용이 있으나 경찰에서 상당히 잘 단속하고 있는것으로 보임. 계속적인 강력한 단속이 필요하며, 미군측에서 수집한 증거를 한국경찰에 통보하여 줄것이 요망됨.

다. 성병 퇴치

동두천과 유사하게 진료소 (4개)및 수용소 (1개소) 가 업태부 (1,700명) 에 비하여 부족함으로 증설이 필요함.

마. 각종 강력범 단속

미군인의 폭음, 습관성 약품의 사용, 업태부에 대한 화대로 인한 시비, 외래품 거래등으로 발생하는 각종 사건을 단속하기 위하여 우범자에 대한 한국경찰의 강력한 단속과

25

미군인에 대한 미 당국의 자체교육이 요망됨.

7. 9. 사건을 비롯하여 각종 사건에 배후관계 (공산당 등)는 없는것으로 보임.

한.미 군,경의 합동순찰을 계속 강화할 것이 요망됨. 부정 외래품의 단속도 한.미 협동으로 계속 강화할 것이 요청되며, 동시에 미측 에서도 외출시 물품 휴대를 극도로 제한할 것이 요망됨.

마. 한.미 친선 협조

한.미 친선협회를 통한 협조가 잘되고 있는것으로 보이나 계속 강화가 요망됨. 한.미 양측이 수립하여 시행하고 있는 대책들은 공히 훌륭한 것으로 보이는바, 그 성과를 거두기에 계속 노력할 것을 권유함.

26

한.미 군민관계 임시 분과위원회

현지 답사 보고

3. 평택군 송탄읍 (1971. 9. 24.)

가. 한.미인 간 충돌문제

(1) 충돌사건의 문제점은 원인면에서는 타 지역과 대동소이하나 2. 15. 의 [redacted] [redacted]의 살인미수 사건을 위시한 미군 병사들중 소수 militant activists 들의 횡포가 유독히 심한곳임. 흑인전용 클럽의 입구에 설치한 선전문및 화보, 클럽안 벽에 칠한 painting (흑인사진과 공산당 선언 같은 "혁명의 때는 왔다", "형제여 뭉쳐라" 는 등등)은 한.미 양국의 우호증진에 악영향을 줄뿐 아니라 이러한 흑인의 극단적이고 독선적인 slogan 은 영업상 큰 장애물이므로 그 철거가 요망됨.

(2) 현재 기지촌 여성들이 패용하고 있는 ribbon 제도에 대한 재고가 있어야 할 것임. 초록, 빨강, 노랑 ribbon 의 표식은 흑인들의

217

한국 여성들에 대한 무차별 대우및 요구를 시정하기 위함이 목적이었으나 초록 (green) 을 다는 여자는 매춘행위에 대한 공식적인 표식임으로 이의 재고가 요청됨.

나. 불매운동 사건

71. 4. 28. K-55 기지 병사들의 위안부 확대 인하 운운하는 유인물 (500매 정도) 살포 사건은 여타 기지에서 볼수없는 특수사건으로 그 방법이 졸렬하고 인권유린 행위로 사료될뿐 아니라 사회의 미풍양속을 해치는 묵과할수 없는 행위로 관계 기지 사령관의 책임있는 답변과 관련 장병에 대한 조치가 요망됨.

다. 마약 단속

타 지역에 비해 큰 문제가 아닌듯함.

라. 성병 퇴치

등록된 위안부 수가 1,100명, 미등록된 수를 합하면 3,000여명에 달함에 비추어 의사 수는 2명에 불과하므로 그 증원이 요청됨.

28

4. 대 구 (1971. 9. 28.)

가. 한.미인 간 충돌사건

(1) 미군 출입 클럽이 대구 시내에 있기 때문에 자연적으로 한국인들의 출입이 잦아, 여기에서 발생하는 충돌사건이 빈번한 곳임.

(2) 한국 경찰측은 미군들의 수준이 주민들의 수준보다 월등히 낮아 사소한 충돌사건이 빈번한바, 구체적인 예로서 9. 11. 흑인 30 - 40명이 집단으로 부대밖을 뛰쳐나와 골목길을 배회하다가 아무런 이유없이 인근 주민에게 돌을 던져 4명의 현지 주민을 부상케 하고 유리 창문을 파손시키는 등 피해를 입혀 주민들의 빈축을 사고 있음.

(3) 또한 한국 경찰측은 사건 관련자에 대한 미 수사기관의 미온적인 처벌이 오히려 사건 발생을 조장한다고 주장하고 사사건건 미군 기지 당국의 철저한 처벌만이 사고 근절책 이라 보고있음.

29

(4) 흑인 militants 의 행동이 두드러지게 심한곳인 바, 그들은 "흑인전용 클럽" (Wanderland)을 선정하고 (this is our territory 라 주장한다고 함.) 백인들의 출입을 일체 금지시킬뿐만 아니라 그 주변일대 클럽에도 백인들의 접근을 위협하고 있어 (if you come to our ~~this~~ border, we will kill you 식으로 위협한다고 함) 영업에도 큰 지장을 초래할뿐 아니라 racial polarization 을 강렬하게 조장하고 있음.

(5) 미군 당국은 최근 발생한 사건 9건중에서 흑인과 한국 여자가 각각 4건이나 관련되었으며, 또한 한번 관련된 병사가 유사한 사건에 계속 관련되었다는 통계로 보아 악질적인 소수의 흑인 militants 가 존재함을 시인하고 이들에 대한 특별한 감시와 교육을 실시할 것이며, 단 극단분자는 타곳으로 전출시킬 계획이라 함.

나. 마약 단속

타 지역에 비해 크게 문제가 되는듯 하지 않음.

70

다. 성병 퇴치

도합 9047명의 검진 연인원 (위안부 4067명, 접대부 4980명) 에 대하여 2명의 의사로서는 효율적인 검진실시가 불가능함으로 의사의 증원이 절실히 요청됨.

마. 각종 강력범 단속

일차적으로 Wanderland club 및 그 인접 우범지대에 유선 통신의 연락망이 가설된 한.미 합동 순찰 초소의 설치가 시급히 요청됨. 특히 흑인 전용 클럽인 Wanderland club 은 그 진입로가 전부 기지촌 민가들로 구성되어 있기 때문에 흑인들의 행패에 인접 주민들은 공포에 떨고있는 실정인 바, 남대구 경찰서장은 민가 보호와 사건 방지에 특별한 책임의식을 갖고 단속반을 강화할 필요가 있음.
미군 기지 사령관은 사건의 99%가 23:00 - 24:00 사이에 발생함을 고려하여 영업 마감시간 30분 전인 23:00 까지는 전원 귀대 조치 또는 외박자는 23:00 이후 일체 길거리를 방황하는 일이 없도록 명령하고 이를 위반하는 자는 강력히 처벌할것.

31

5. 인천, 부평 (1971. 9. 30.)

가. 한.미인 간 충돌사건

(1) 부대이동으로 인한 부채 미청산에 따른 충돌 사건이 최근 빈번하였음.

(2) 또한 전년도에 비해 폭력사건이 증가 일로에 있을뿐만 아니라 그 폭행의 방법이 잔인의 극에 달한바, 그 실례로서 8. 29. ██████ ██████ 병장이 행한 위안부 학대 사건임. 약술하면 자정이 가까운 시간에 가해자 ██████ 병장이 피해자 █████의 집에 침입하여 독약(미상)을 포도주에 타서 먹이고 강약을 실신 시킨후 추행한뒤 국부에 큰 상처를 입힌바 있음. 상기 위안부 학대사건을 위시해서 방화사건, 집단 음주 폭행사건등의 폭력행위로 기지촌 주민들로 부터 크게 빈축을 사고 있는바, 한.미 양국 관계자들의 공동노력이 시급히 요청되고 있음.

나. 마약 단속

마약, 특히 대마초 (marijuana)의 사용자가

32

증가 일로에 있는 바, 집중적인 마약단속을 위해 한.미 관계 책임자들의 공동노력이 요청되고 있음.

다. 각종 강력범 단속

(1) 미 헌병이 한국인 피의자를 조사할 때 한국인을 미군 영내로 동행 심문하는 예가 종종 있다는 바, 미군 기지 사령관은 이러한 일이 재발치 않도록 철저히 조치할 것이며, 한국인 피의자를 즉시 한국 수사기관에 이첩해서 심문토록 해야 할 것임.

(2) 폭력사건의 예방조치로서 미군 기지 당국은 사병들의 야간 외출시간을 23:00 까지로 강력한 통제가 요망됨.

(3) 미군 기지 당국은 미군 상사단으로 자체 감찰반을 조직하여 매일 야간에 정복 착용, 각 클럽을 수시 감찰시킴이 요청됨.

6. 군 산 (1971. 10. 7.)

가. 한.미인 간 충돌사건

(1) 한국 경찰측 "브리핑"에 의하면 타 기지에 비해 병사들의 수준 (미 공군 전투부대)은 낮지않으나, 위안부들의 교육수준이 월등히 낮다는 것임.
부대안에서의 흑백 군인 대립 감정이 한국 위안부 상호간의 감정 대립을 초래하고, 위안부 끼리의 감정 대립은 그들이 사귀는 흑백 군인들 간의 감정을 격화하는 소위 연쇄반응적인 대립 현상이 잠재하고 있고, 위안부들의 자기 이익 추구를 위한 무분별 행동으로 충돌사건이 비교적 잦은곳임.

(2) Silver Town 의 성공적인 경영은 타 기지에 비해 특기할 사항임. 입지적으로 부대에 인접해 있는 이 "독립 마을" 은 기지 사령관과의 긴밀한 협조하에 미군 병사들의 욕구에 최대의 Service 를 제공하고 합리적인 관리를 함으로서 기지촌의 한.미인 간 유대 강화에 관건이 되고있음.

34

(3) 또한 미군기지 사령관의 정책으로 Sault & Pepper Team 이 대활약중에 있어, 한.미인간 충돌사건 예방에 임익을 담당하고 있음.

(4) 그러나 사건 처리 과정에서 한.미 관계자들의 무성의와 비협조가 나타나고 있는듯 함. 즉, 4. 25 미 헌병이 저지른 ████ 살해 사건은 한국 정부에서 이의를 제기할수 있는 충분한 소제가 있었음에도 불구하고 아무런 이의 제기도 없이 지방경찰서 "레벨"에서 유야무야 처리되었으며, 동시에 미측에서는 사건 처리 결과도 한국측에 통보하지 않았고 한국측에서도 추후 요구하지도 않았음. 그래서 한국측 지방관서에서는 그 사건의 공정 처리 여부에 대한 파악을 못하고 있었으며, 미군 피의자가 무죄 석방되었다는 사실은 현지 시찰중에 한국측 분과위원들의 추궁에 의해 비로서 알게 되었음.

나. 성 병

Silver Town 의 성공적인 운영으로 타 지역에 비해 크게 문제되는 점은 아니나, 성병문제의 주안점은

35

Street Walker(Name Card 가 없으며, 등록치 않고 미군을 상대하는 위안부)를 강력히 통제하는데 있음. 즉, 정확한 Street Walker 수의 파악과 이들로 하여금 등록하여 주기적인 검진을 받도록 할것이며, 이에 불응하는 위안부는 미군을 상대하지 못하도록 강력 통제하여야 할 것임.

36

기 안 용 지

분류기호 문서번호	미이723-	(전화번호)	전결규정 조항 국장 전결사항
처리기간			
시행일자	71. 11. 11.		
보존년한			국 장

보조기관	북미2과장		협조
기안책임자	권 찬	북미2과 (71. 11. 11.)	

경유 수신 참조	장 관 (수신처 관계장관) 한.미 합동위원회 군.민관계 분과위원회 위원
제목	부산 ~~미군 기지촌~~ 현지답사 계획 통보

발송 No. 2548 1971. 11. 11. 외무부

검열 1971. 11. 11. 통제관

한.미 합동위원회 군민관계 임시분과위원회가 하기와같은 계획으로 부산을 현지 답사키로 되었아오니 필히 참여토록 하여주시기 바랍니다.

11. 14.	14:00	서울출발
		헤리콥터 또는 U-21기 (미측 제공)
	15:30	부산 도착
		유 숙 (자 유)
11. 15.	09:00 - 11:00	부산시청에서 청문회
	11:00 - 12:00	기지촌 답사
	12:30 - 13:30	오 찬 (미측 초대)
	13:30 - 15:30	미 기지에서 청문회
	16:00 -	부산 출발
	17:30	서울 도착 끝.

정서 / 관인 / 발송

공통서식 1-2 (갑)
1967. 4. 4 승인

190mm×268mm 중질지 70g/m²
조달청 (1,000,000매 인쇄)

27

외 무 부

미이 723 -　　　　　　　　　　　　　　　　71. 11. 11.

수신 :

참조 :

제목 : 부산 현지답사 계획 통보

한.미 합동위원회 군.민관계 임시분과위원회가 아래와같은 계획으로 부산을 현지답사키로 되었아오니 필히 참여토록 하여주시기 바랍니다.

11.	14.	14:00	서울 출발
			헤리콥터 또는 U-21 기(미측 제공)
		15:30	부산 도착
			유 숙(자 유)
11.	15.	09:00 - 11:00	부산시청에서 청문회
		11:00 - 12:00	기지촌 답사
		12:30 - 13:30	오 찬(미측 초대)
		13:30 - 15:30	미 기지에서 청문회
		16:00 -	부산 출발
		17:30	서울 도착 끝.

외 무 부 장 관

38

Proposed Schedule for Pusan, 15 November 1971

0930 - 1100	ROK officials discussion at City Hall.
1100 - 1200	Tour of Bar Area.
1230 - 1330	Lunch at Officers Club, Hialeah Compound.
1330 - 1530	Discussion with Military authorities at Hialeah Compound. (Conference Room, 2nd Trans Gp).

39

DISPOSITION FORM

For use of this form, see AR 340-15; the proponent agency is The Adjutant General's Office.

REFERENCE OR OFFICE SYMBOL	SUBJECT
USFK EJ	Request for Army Aviation Support

TO CG, EUSA
ATTN: Aviation Section

FROM CAPT Romanick

DATE 9 Nov 71
LTC KOLDITZ/rlh/3102

CMT 1

1. Request helicopter support for 12 US and ROK members of the Ad Hoc Subcommittee on Civil-Military Relations to Pusan and return on 14 and 15 November 1971, respectively. The Subcommittee will meet with ROK city officials and US commanders, and visit city recreational areas.

2. Itinerary:

Sunday, 14 November 1971: Depart H-201 - 1400 hours.
Arrive K-9 - 1530 hours.

Monday, 15 November 1971: Depart K-9 - 1600 hours.
Arrive H-201 - 1730 hours.

3. This is the seventh fact-finding trip by the Subcommittee.

4. Two U-21 aircraft preferred, if available.

Friday
5 - 6-6

F M Romanick
F. M. ROMANICK
CAPT USN
US Chairman
Ad Hoc Subcommittee on
Civil-Military Relations

COORDINATION:

DCS, EUSA----Concur

Kenney, Leonard Alan Kikdong

40

DA FORM 1 FEB 62 2496 REPLACES DD FORM 96, EXISTING SUPPLIES OF WHICH WILL BE ISSUED AND USED UNTIL

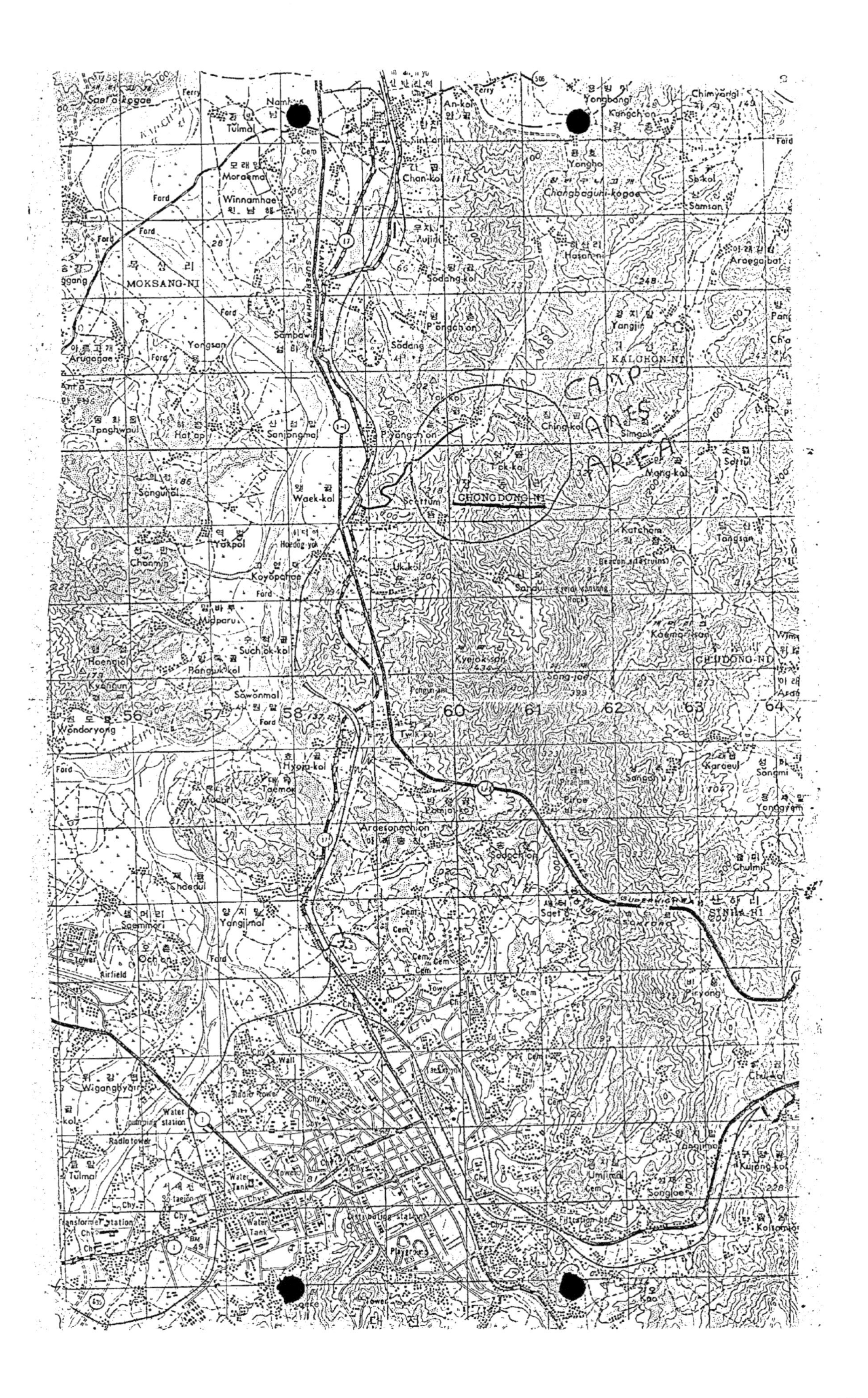
CAMP AMES AREA
CHONGDONG-NI
MOKSANG-NI
KALCHON-NI
CHUDONG-NI

기지촌 정화를 위한 외무부 시행계획

I. 시행중인 사항

1. 성병 관리

가. SOFA 제 69차 합동회의 (71. 12. 16.)에서 성병의 원인 제거와 기지촌 한국 "크럽" 변소 시설의 위생개선에 대하여 각각 건의서를 채택, 통과시키고, 이를 관계부처가 시행중에 있음.

나. SOFA 제 69차 회의에서 합의, 채택된 사항 :

(1) (가) 성병예방을 담당하는 한.미 관계당국은 성병 보균자로 하여금 치료토록하고 완치될때까지 공중으로부터 격리할것.

(나) 한국 관계당국과 미군당국은 성병의 원인제거 및 예방에 관한 교육 계획을 함께세울것.

(2) 한국 보건당국은 기지촌 한국 "크럽" 소유자에게 다음과 같은 긴급조치를 취하도록 할것.

(가) 변소의 세척물이 적절히 나오도록 함.

(나) 변소에 수건, 종이등을 비치토록 함.

(다) 변기세척, 청소 및 종이나 수건을 제공하는 사람을 배치토록 함.

42

2. APO 기관 강화

가. 외무부는 SOFA 합동위 산하 군.민관계 임시분과위원회에 마약단속을 위한 APO 기관 강화에 대한 과제를 위촉한바 있으며, 분과위원회에서 이를 채택하고 합동위원회에서 합의되는대로 그 시행을 촉구할것임 :

과제위촉 내용 : 마약 및 습관성 의약품의 APO 를 통한 반입을 방지하기 위하여 현재 10 %로 되어 있는 소포검사 제도 와는 관계없이 과학적 방법, 경찰견등을 이용하여 한.미 합동으로 적발한다.

나. 뿐만아니라 SOFA 합동위 재무분과위원회의 활동을 강화하여 APO 를 통한 마약 및 밀수범 단속에 더욱 박차를 가할것임.

3. PX 유출품 단속 강화

미군병사의 외출시 휴대 허용품을 제한하도록 하기위한 과제를 합동위 군.민관계 임시분과위원회에 위촉하였음.

과제위촉 내용 : PX 유출품 (세금 면제된채) 이 한국경제에 미치는 악영향을 고려하여 미군병사의 외출시 휴대허용품 (예 : 맥주 1상자등)을 축소 (minimize), 제한 (restrict) 하도록 미측에 촉구한다.

43

4. 한.미 친선협의회 운영 강화

SOFA 합동위 제 68차회의 (71. 11. 24.)에서 한.미 양국이 한.미 친선협의회 (The Korean American Friendship Councils)를 신설할것을 합의하고, 지역문제의 원만한 해결과 상호 우의를 위하여 각지역의 적정한 "레벨" 에서 한.미 친선협의회를 조직할것을 결의, 동 과시킨바 있음.

양국간의 상위 "레벨"에서뿐만 아니라, 도, 시 단위의 각지역 "레벨"에서 친선협의회가 조직되면 실질적인 성과를 기대할수 있을것임.

5. 미군표 교환소 증설

한.미 군대지위협정 제 19조 2항에 의하여 미군은 군표를 관리하기 위하여 대한민국의 상업금융업체 (Korean Commercial Banking Business)로부터 격리된곳에 군표교환소를 설치할수 있게되어있는바, 외무부는 미 당국에 아래와같이 군표교환소의 증설과 교환의 편리를 도모케하도록 요청할것임.

가. 군영문에 교환소를 상설한다.

나. 관광업소 집중지대 인근에 교환소를 상설한다.

6. AFKN-TV 시간 할애

가. 2월 9일 한.미 군대지위협정 발효 제 5주년 기념일에 즈음하여 주한미군의 고유프로로서 SOFA 합동위 양측대표 (외무부

44

김동휘 구미국장 및 Smith 중장)의 AFKN-TV 출연과 2월 중순경 군.민관계 임시분과위 양측 위원장(외무부 김영섭 과장 및 Romanick 대령)의 TV 출연을 계획하고 있음.

나. 추후의 이용도를 높이기 위하여 외무부는 SOFA 합동위의 의제로 상정하여 필요시에 항시 이용할수 있도록 협의할것임.

45

II. 계획중인 사항

1. 인천 상담소 설치

2. 사격장 관리 협조

3. 한.미 합동 작업훈련

4. 한.미 합동 의료평가

5. 주기적인 역학 치료

6. 군수품의 오물처리

이상의 계획중인 사업을 위해서는,

가. SOFA Channel 을 통하여 미측과 협의하고, 최대의 협조를 할것이며,

나. 또한 SOFA 합동위를 더욱 강화하여 어려운 문제는 의제로 채택, 해결할 방침임.

46

5-1 基地村 對策

基本方向

1. 全國 48個 基地村 環境淨化 및 福祉增進
2. 各部處의 施策을 綜合調整

推進計劃

1. 韓美親善紐帶强化——韓美親善委員會 月 1回以上 開催

(韓國側)	(美軍側)
知　事	: 軍團長
郡　守(警察署長包含)	: 師團長 : 旅團長
邑面長(支署長包含)	: 部隊長

2. 保健對策事業

- ○ 衛生檢察徹底————————合同檢査班
- ○ 施設環境改善(接客業所)——照明, 美化, 水洗式施設
- ○ 性病檢疫徹底————————診療所의 適正運營

3. 社會淨化事業

- ○ 淪落女性善導(自治會活用)—集團化아파트建立, 職業輔導
- ○ 住民의 意識轉換————黑人差等 생각拂拭
- ○ 痲藥, 幻覺劑————————源泉惡 塞源
- ○ 暴力, 盜犯 및 强力根絕——防犯合同巡察班(部落單位)

— 96 —

47

4. 環境改善事業

○ 基地村進入路 鋪裝

○ 뒷골목改修 鋪裝, 步道부럭 깔기

○ 保安(街路)燈 設置

5. 事業遂行要領

○ 地域別 優先順位 策定施行

○ 事業別 優先順位 策定施行

○ 責任擔當制 實施

○ 事業計劃 報告 1. 29까지

※參照 ○外國軍基地村 淨化對策指示(大秘政 110-115, 71. 12. 31)

○ 48個基地村一覽表

548

Mr. Smorhers, ladies and gentlemen:

I should like to briefly outline the base community clean-up projects being implemented by the Government of the Republic of Korea for the amelioration of environmental conditions of the Korean communities adjacent to the US military installations, and for the improvement of civil-military relations between the US military personnel and Koreans living in the camp communities.

President Park, after an inspection tour of I Corps last December, directed his political secretary to come up with a relevant and comprehensive plan that will purify all the problems related to the camp communities. First step taken in this regard was the organization of the "Base Community Clean-up Committee" which is composed of Vice Ministers of the Ministries of Foreign Affairs, Home Affairs, Justice, National Defense, Health and Social Welfare, Transportation, and Culture and Public Information, Director of

Customs Office, Governer of Kyunggi-do, Deputy Vice Minister of the Economic Planning Board, and Political Secretary to the Prime Minister. The Committee is headed by the Senior Political Secretary to the President. The functions of this Committee is to review and coordinate all the plans and projects submitted by the ministries concerned, making recommendations to the President for approval.

The Committee on the outset determined the problem areas in civil-military affairs, and consolidated each plan submitted by the ministries and ~~affairs~~ offices concerned into a grand master plan. Projects contained in this master plan fall into five categories, that is, the social projects, the health and sanitation projects, the environmental purification projects, the goodwill activities projects and the livelihood projects.

The social projects encompasses such areas as encroachment, maintenance of law and order, larceny and black-marketing, law enforcement, racial discrimination and accommodation of special entertainers.

The health and sanitation include drugs and narcotics, VD control. sanitation of tourist facilities and streets, and prevention of tuberculosis.

The environmental purification is intended for improvement of road, sanitary facilities, street lighting and housing.

The goodwill activities comprise operation of local friendship council, public relations and cultural exchange activities.

The livelihood projects covers such areas as poverty program, vocational training, and cultivation of forward area for farming, planting and breeding of domestic animals.

The budget requirement for entire projects is assessed by the Committee Secretariat at some 1.15 billion won which is equivalent to almost 3 million US dollars. This amount was not earmarked in the budget of the current year since these new projects were established after the national assembly had passed the 1972 budget.

Now the Korean Government is considering a supplemental budget for this purpose. However, by transfering the budget for other projects of lower priorities, the required money is expected to be secured.

These various projects are now underway with a remarkable progress in some areas and a slow but steady progress in other areas. Korean Government is doing its utmost to achieve the goal set by the President, so that the U.S. Forces in Korea can enjoy better environment while they are stationed here.

Pubwon-Ni, Cp. Irwin Live Within Limits of Friendship

SLS 71.12.29

By SPEC. 4 DENNIS LATTA

PUBWON-NI, Korea (Special) — Like the eye of a hurricane, quiet little Pubwon-Ni village, outside the main gate to Camp Irwin, sits in the midst of off-limits villages but remains trouble-free.

Camp Irwin serves as the administrative area for both B and C Batteries of the 2nd Bn., 71st Air Defense Arty., but it is also surrounded by units of the 2nd Inf. Div.

Recently, area villages were placed off-limits by the 2nd Division, but Pubwon-Ni remains on-limits.

Problems closed the other villages but "we haven't had any real problems here," explained C Battery's first sergeant, Sgt. 1. C. James Thomas.

The men at Camp Irwin credit the community relations program there for creating the friendly atmosphere among the Koreans and Americans.

"I'd say our program is successful because of what we've been able to do for the Korean people," said Capt. Lawrence Brotherton, B Btry., commander and president of the Community Relations Advisory Council at Camp Irwin.

"We're a smaller unit so we've been working closer," he explained.

According to Thomas, "We're continually hauling things for the local Koreans . . . We hauled 70 loads of sand to the primary school, hay for the village and a few weeks ago we hauled about 500 local school children to an athletic event at Kwan-Ton."

Because of the efforts the men at Irwin have made for the community, local Koreans reciprocate by working closely with Brotherton and the CRAC council.

"When we have any problems in the village, any trouble, they come directly to me," said Brotherton.

"When a man tears something up, he has to pay for it. We stress that every man here is nothing more than an ambassador . . . through him the Korean people view the whole United States."

No military police are used to patrol the village at Irwin because "everyone here is on the honor system," pointed out the Bravo Battery BC. "The men take care of each other and the presence of an MP sometimes makes the men uncomfortable. The CQs from both batteries walk through the village once a night and that's always been enough."

But since the other villages in the area have been placed off-limits, the population of fun-seeking GI's in Pubwon-Ni increases nightly and now the 2nd Div. is sending its MPs to patrol the village on Camp Irwin's outskirts.

Korean representatives on the Camp Irwin CRAC council include the village mayor, the two school principals, a doctor, a club representative and the local police chief.

"When these other villages were placed off-limits, I warned the CRAC council that more men would be coming to the village. But if we do have trouble in Pubwon-Ni, I'll probably know about it before the MPs do," believes Brotherton.

53

정/리/보/존/문/서/목/록

기록물종류	문서-일반공문서철	등록번호	10936 11244	등록일자	93-09-06
분류번호	729.419	국가코드		주제	
문서철명	SOFA 한.미국 합동위원회 군민관계 임시분과위원회 설치(1971.9.2) - 한국 민간인과 주한 미군간의 충돌사건 방지 대책. 1971				
생산과	북미2과	생산년도	1971 - 1971	보존기간	영구
담당과(그룹)	미주	안보		서가번호	--
참조분류					
권차명					
내용목차	* 1971.9.2 군민관계 임시분과위원회를 합동위원회의 실무기관으로 설치합의. - 7.9. 흑인 병사와 평택 주민간의 충돌사건 및 8.18 동두천 주민 150명과 미군 헌병 80명간의 투석전 등 충돌 재발 방지 조치				

마/이/크/로/필/름/사/항

촬영연도	*롤 번호	화일 번호	후레임 번호	보관함 번호
2007-9	Re-07-10	10	167	

1

(国務会議 報告資料)

71.8.31.

駐韓美軍과 韓国人의 衝突事件

1. 問題点

가. 経緯

1) 平沢事件

7月9日 平沢에서 発生한 黑人兵士와 現地住民들 間의 衝突事件은 黑人에 対한 韓国人의 人種差別이 原因인 것이 外信에 報道되어 美国에서 物議를 이르켰고 一部 黑人議員들은 (Dellums 의원등) 韓国人의 黑人差別待遇를 猛烈히 非難하고 韓国에 対한 美国의 援助中断을 主張하기에 이르렀음.

2) 政府措置

外務部는 駐美各公館에 訓令하여 当該議員 및 主要言論機関을 相対로 実情을 알리고 解明하도록 措置하는 한便, 韓美合同委에서 事件의 收拾 및 再発의 防止策을 協議하고 있으며 8月 18日에는 当部 主宰下에 関係部処 実務者会議를 召集하여 原因分析 및 対策을 検討하였음.

~1~

나. 展望.

美軍의 數는 減少되고 있으나 美軍이 関聯된 事件의 發生件數는 昨年度에 比하여 近 倍增하였으며 黑.白紛糾의 悪化, 美軍內 紀律의 弛緩等 諸現象에 비추어 볼 때 이러한 趨勢는 継続될것으로 보임.

1). 韓美関係에 미칠 悪影響

이러한 事件의 再發은 앞으로도 人種問題와 結付되어 報道되므로서 美議会内의 所謂 Black Caucus를 刺戟하여 美国의 対韓政策에 対한 不利한 圧力으로 나타날것이며 特히 海外駐屯 美軍의 撤収를 要求하는 美国內 輿論이 高潮되고 있는 現時点에서 韓美関係 全般에 걸쳐 좋지 않은 影響을 미칠 憂慮가 있음.

2). 基地周辺住民의 被害.

韓美間의 衝突事件이 美国內에서 政治問題化 되고 있는 傾向에 비추어 駐韓美軍当局은 事件의 予防을 為하여 強硬措置를 不辞하고 있는바. 事件 發生地域에 対한 美軍의 出入禁止令等은 基地 周辺 住民의 生計를 威脅하고 있음.

2-1

2. 対策

가. 対策樹立의 時急性.

人種問題를 内包하는 韓美間의 衝突事件은 美国社会의 人種紛糾가 韓国 땅에 移植되어서 発生한 事件이지만 그 原因에 対하여는 韓美間에 多少 立場의 差異가 있으며 結果的으로는 우리에게 不利한 事態이므로 이를 未然에 防止하기 為한 対策樹立이 時急함.

나. 韓美 軍民関係 分科委의 設置

그間 外務部에서는 韓美合同委를 通하여 美側과 対策을 協議하여 왔으나, 問題의 根本的 解決을 為하여는 基地周辺地域에서 뿐만 아니라 中央에서도 韓美間의 緊密한 協力이 必要하며 또한 政府関係部処의 共同努力이 必須的인바 이 目的을 為하여 韓美合同委의 実務機関으로서 軍民関係分科委 (ad hoc Subcommittee for Civil-Military Relations)를 設置할 것에 意見을 合했음.

3

다. 分科委의 機能.

同 分科委에서는 駐韓美軍과 基地周辺住民間의 問題뿐만 아니라 美軍部隊에 勤務하는 韓国人 從業員과 美軍間의 諸問題도 아울러 다루게 하므로써 美軍과 韓国民間人 間에 発生하는 모든 問題의 解決策을 合同委에 建議하는 任務를 遂行하게 될 것임.

라. 分科委의 構成

同 分科委의 運用을 通하여 所期의 成果를 거두려면 外務部, 法務部, 内務部, 交通部, 保社部 그리고 労働庁이 参与 하여야 할 것인바, 該当部処에서는 外務部의 要請에 따라 委員을 任命하여 주시고 問題의 重大性에 鑑하여 次後 分科委 任務遂行에 最大限으로 協力하여 주시기 바람.

<u>参考資料</u>

1. 美国内의 反響

가. 平沢事件에 対한 AP 報道 (7.10) 를 美国新聞들이 揭載

나. 美下院 外務委 Executive Session 에서 黑人 議員들이 韓国人의 人種差別 非難 発言 (7.14)

다. Dellums 下院議員 談話 発表 (7.15.)

라. Mitchell 下院議員의 非難 発言 (7.19. Baltimore Sun)

마. Black Caucus 連判状 (7.22)

바. 국무장관의 在外公館長앞 訓令 (8.27.)

2. 政府措置.

가. 駐美各公館에 対한 訓令 (7.19.)

나. 駐美大使館 公報官의 解明 書翰 揭載

Washington Post (7.17.)

Evening Star (7.20.)

다. 韓美合同委 上程 (7.29.)

3. 駐韓美軍의 措置.

가. 対民関係 改善에 関한 政策指示 下達 (7.15.)

나. 平沢 安井里 出入禁止. — 48日間

다. 東豆川 턱거리 出入禁止令 (8.18.)

- 1. -

5

4. 駐韓美軍 犯罪統計.

1970年 480件.

1971年 上半期 467件.

5. 觀光休養業所 現況

全國 總 214個所.

平澤地域 (71.6.30 現在) (70.6.30 現在)

	(71.6.30 現在)	(70.6.30 現在)
美軍總數	4.632.	5.305
韓國接客業所	20	19
慰安婦數	2.490	1.685.

6. 原因分析.

가. 美軍側 主張

1). 黑白 兵士가 出入하는 클럽이 各各 區分되어 있다.

2). 一部 클럽에서는 業主, 從業員이 黑人을 差別待遇 한다.

가). 音樂選擇에 黑人嗜好 無視

나). 黑人要請에 對한 慰安婦의 不應

3). 基地 周辺地域에서의 韓國官憲의 統制 및 對美協助가 微溫的이다.

가). 性病의 蔓延과 麻薬의 出廻

나). 住民의 対美軍暴行 傍観

다). 基地 司令官의 面談要請 黙殺

라). 廢业 滋谷 附近 部隊 周辺에는 韓国官憲 不在

나. 韓国人側 主張

1). 黑白 差別의 区分은 美軍自身들의 選択의 結果이다.

2). 黑人에 対한 差別은 白人兵士의 黑人에 対한 人種意識의 反映에 不過하다

가). 黑人音樂이 나오면 白人은 退去

나). 黑人과 接触한 慰安婦는 白人이 不相從

3). 数的으로 적은 (10:1) 黑人은 消費가 적은 反面 一般的으로 暴悪하다.

4). 性病의 蔓延은 未登録 慰安婦를 美軍營内에 自由로이 出入시키는데 基因한다.

— 3 —

7

지급

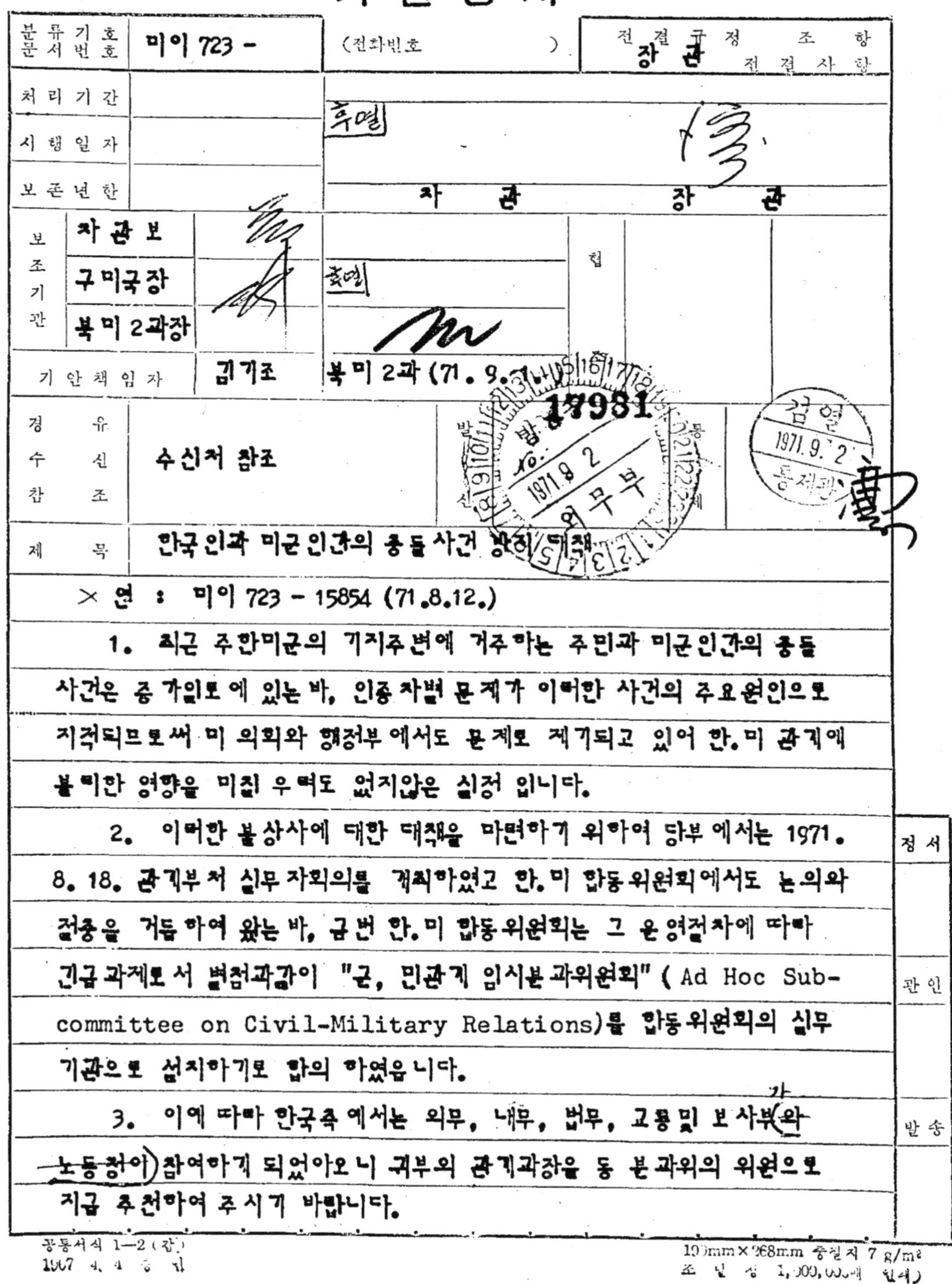

기 안 용 지

분류기호 문서번호	미이 723 -	(전화번호)	전결규정 조항 장관 전결사항
처리기간			
시행일자		후열	
보존년한		차관	장관
보조기관	차관보		협조
	구미국장	후열	
	북미 2과장		
기안책임자	김기조	북미 2과 (71. 9. 1)	
경유 수신 참조	수신처 참조		
제목	한국인과 미군인간의 충돌사건 방지 대책		

발신 1971.9.2 외무부 17981

검열 1971.9.2 통제관

× 연 : 미이 723 - 15854 (71.8.12.)

1. 최근 주한미군의 기지주변에 거주하는 주민과 미군인간의 충돌사건은 증가일로에 있는 바, 인종차별 문제가 이러한 사건의 주요원인으로 지적되므로써 미 의회와 행정부에서도 문제로 제기되고 있어 한.미 관계에 불리한 영향을 미칠 우려도 없지않은 실정 입니다.

2. 이러한 불상사에 대한 대책을 마련하기 위하여 당부에서는 1971. 8. 18. 관계부처 실무자회의를 개최하였고 한.미 합동위원회에서도 논의와 절충을 거듭하여 왔는 바, 금번 한.미 합동위원회는 그 운영절차에 따라 긴급과제로서 별첨과같이 "군, 민관계 임시분과위원회" (Ad Hoc Sub-committee on Civil-Military Relations)를 합동위원회의 실무기관으로 설치하기로 합의 하였읍니다.

3. 이에 따라 한국측에서는 외무, 내무, 법무, 교통및 보사부가 ~~와 노동청이~~ 참여하게 되었아오니 귀부의 관계과장을 동 분과위의 위원으로 지급 추천하여 주시기 바랍니다.

정서
관인
발송

공통서식 1—2 (갑)
1967. 4. 4 승인

190mm×268mm 중질지 7 g/m²
조달청 1,000,000매 인쇄)

별첨 : 합동위원회 각서 사본 1 부. 끝

수신처 : 내무부장관 (치안국장) (지방국장)
법무부장관 (검찰국장)
교통부장관 (관광국장)
보건사회부장관 (보건국장)
(노동청장 (노정국장))

공 란

한국인과 미군인간의 충돌사건 방지대책

공문 접수 서명란.

1. 내무부장관	치안국장	[signature] 9. 2.
	지방국장.	[signature]
2. 법무부장관	검찰국장	[signature]
3. 교통부 장관	관광국장	[signature]
4. 보사부 장관	보건국장.	[signature]

11

교 통 부

진흥 1530 -1183 1971. 9. 2

수신 외무부장관

제목 군,민 관계 임시분과 합동위원회 위원 추천

미이 723 - 17981 (71. 9. 1)에 의한 군,민 관계 임시분과 합동위원회 위원으로 당부 관계관 추천 요청에 대하여 다음과 같이 알립니다.

추천자 : 관광국 진흥과장 김 철 용 끝.

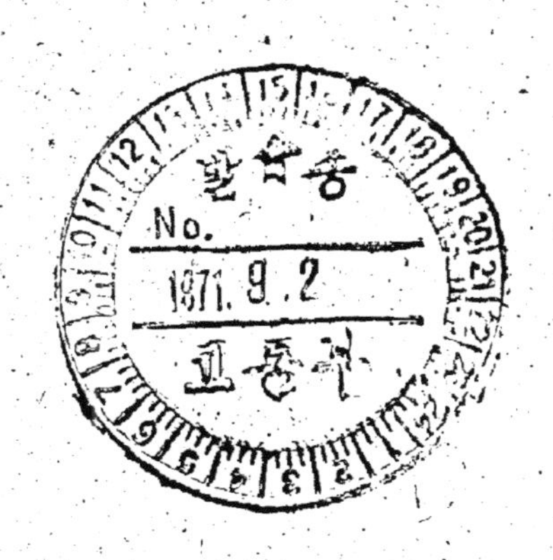

교 통 부 장

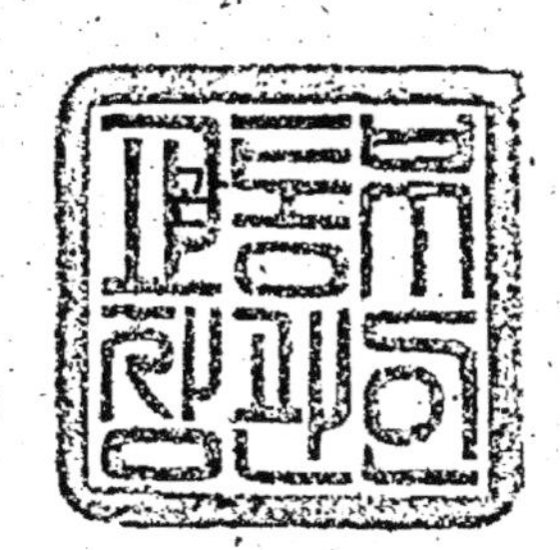

12

외 무 부		결재		
접수 일시	197 . . . 시 SEP	지시사항	9 : 30	
접수 번호	제 36556 호			
주무과				
담당자			197 . . . 까지 처리할 것	
결				

법 무 부

검찰 821- 15932 73-7942 1971. 9. 3.

수신 외무부장관

참조 구미국장

제목 한국인과 미군인간의 충돌사건 방지 대책

미이 723-17981(71. 9. 2)에 의거 아래사람을 선정 추천 합니다.

아 래

직위	성명	비고
검사	현홍주	형사분위
검사	정구영	민사분위. 끝.

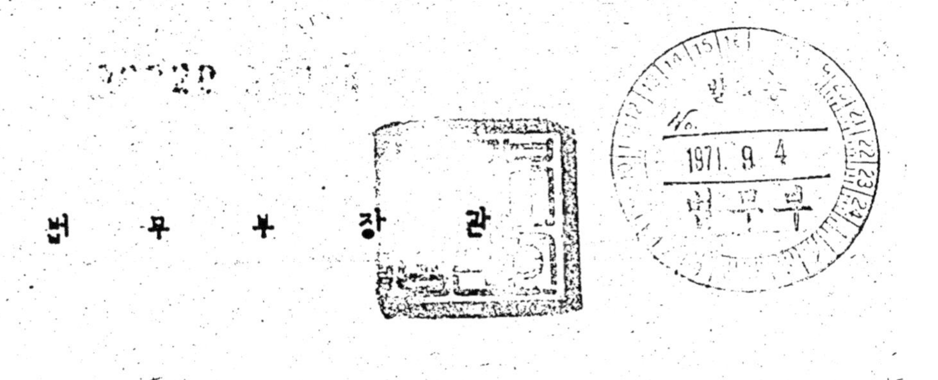

법 무 부 장 관

13

외 무 부		결재	
접수 일시	197SEP 11 시 분	지시	
접수 번호	제 36851		
주무과			
담당자			
처리 근거			197 . . 까지 처리할 것

내 무 부

관리 723-8074 (22.2342) 1971. 9. 4

수 신 외무부장관

참 조 미주국장

제 목 군민관계 임시분과 위원회 위원 추천 회신

1. 미이 723-17981 (71. 9. 1)의 응신입니다.

2. 군민관계 임시분과 위원회 위원으로 당부 관리과장을 추천합니다.

가. 직 급 서 기 관

나. 성 명 백 세 현 끝

내 무 부 장 관

14

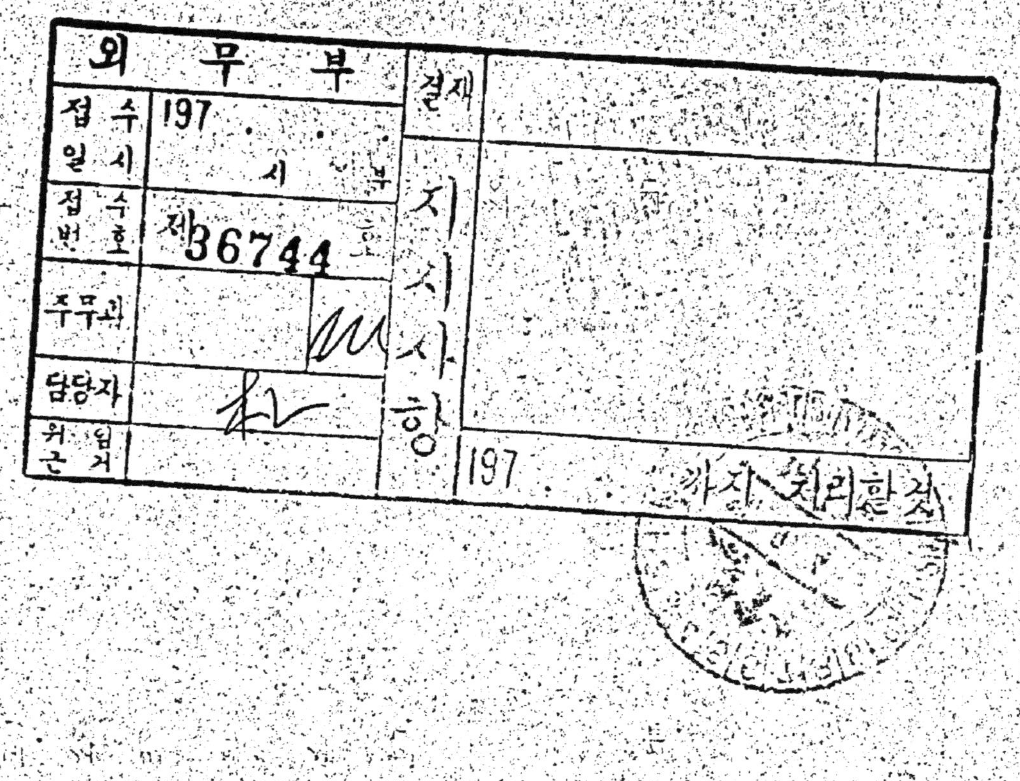

외무부		결재	
접수일시	197 . . . 시 분	지시사항	
접수번호	제36744호		
주무과			
담당자			
위임근거			197 . . . 까지 처리할 것

내 무 부

외사 2068 - 6457 1971. 9. 4.

수신 외무부 장관

참조 구 미 국 장

제목 한국인과 미군인간의 충돌사건 방지 대책

1. 미이 723 - 17981 (71. 9. 1.) 과 관련된것임.

2. 한국인과 미군인간의 충돌사건 방지 대책을 위하여 설치되는 "군.민 관계 임시분과 위원회" 위원을 다음과 같이 2명을 추천 통보합니다.

내무부 치안국 외사과장 경무관 김 봉 군.

" " 외사 3담당 총 경 이 ... 끝.

내 무 부 장 관

15

외 무 부		결재		
접수일시	197 7 SEP 시 분	지시사항		
접수번호	제 36857 호			
주무과				
담당자				
위임근거			197 . . .까지 처리할것	

공 란

공 란

공 란

공 란

공 란

공 란

공 란

공 란

공 란

공 란

공 란

공 란

기 안 용 지

분류기호 문서번호	미이 723 -	(전화번호)	전결규정 조 항 장관 전결사항
처리기간			
시행일자	71. 9. 4.		
보존년한		차 관	장 관
보조기관	차관보		협
	구미국장		
	북미 2과장		
기안책임자	김기조	북미 2과 (71. 9. 4.)	
경유 수신 참조	대통령각하 (사본 : 외무담당 특별보좌관) 국무총리각하	발신 18367 1971. 9. 6 외무부	통제 1971. 9. 6
제목	한국 민간인과 미국 군인간의 충돌사건 방지 대책		

연 : 미이 723 - 14084 (71. 7. 27. 자, 평택사건)

연호로 보고한바있는 평택사건과 관련하여 주한 미대사관 Underhill 공사는 9. 1. 본직을 방문하여 별첨과 같은 흑인출신 미 하원의원들의 닉슨 대통령 앞 연판장 (한국에서와 같은 흑백 차별대우를 근절시키는 강력한 조치를 요청함) 과 로저스 국무장관이 미국군이 주둔하는 지역의 전 재외공관장에게 차별대우 해소를 위하여 가능한 조치를 취하라고 지시한 문서 (사본) 를 제시하면서, 아국정부의 가능한 조치와 협조를 요청하여 왔읍니다. 당부는 이와같은 한국 민간인과 미군인간의 충돌사건의 경위, 원인분석, 전망, 및 대책등을 8.31 ~~이미 국무회의에 보고하였으며 미군측과 협조를 (한 …) 하여 충돌대책을 수립중~~ 있는바. 그 내용을, 다음과 같이 보고 합니다.

1. 사건 경위

가. 평택 사건

7월 9일 평택에서 발생한 흑인병사와 현지 주민들간의 충돌사건은 흑인에 대한 한국인의 인종 차별이 원인인듯이 외신에 보도되어 미국에서 물의를 이르켰고 일부 흑인의원

정서 | 관인 | 발송

공통서식 1—2 (갑)
1967. 4. 4 승인

190mm×268mm 중질지 7 g/m²
조 달 청 1,000,000매 인쇄)

- 28

들은 한국인의 흑인 차별대우를 맹렬히 비난하고 한국에 대한 미국의 원조 중단을 주장하기에 이르렀음.

나. 8. 18. 밤 동두천 미 제2사단 정문앞에서 주민 약 150명과 미 헌병 80명이 대치, 투석전이 있었음. 이는 미 병사와 위안부간의 사소한 언쟁으로 발단, 순경과 미 헌병 1명간의 언쟁으로 발전, 확대된 사건임.

2. 원인 분석

가. 미군측 주장

(1) 흑백병사가 출입하는 클럽이 각각 구분되어 있다.

(2) 일부 클럽에서는 업주, 종업원이 흑인을 차별대우 한다.

(가) 음악선택에 흑인기호 무시

(나) 흑인 요청에 대한 위안부의 불응

(3) 기지주변 지역에서의 한국 관헌의 통제및 대미협조가 미온적이다.

(가) 성병의 만연과 마약의 출회

(나) 주민의 대 미군 폭행의 방관

(다) 기지 사령관의 면담요청 묵살

나. 한국측 주장

(1) 흑백클럽의 구분은 미군 자신들의 선택의 결과이다.

(2) 흑인에 대한 차별은 백인병사의 흑인에 대한 인종의식의 반영에 불과하다.

(가) 흑인 음악이 나오면 백인은 퇴거

(나) 흑인과 접촉한 위안부는 백인 불상대

(3) 숫적으로 적은 (10:1)흑인은 소비가 적은 반면, 일반적으로 포악하다.

27

3. 전 망

미군의 수는 감소되고 있으나, 미군이 관련된 사건의 발생건수는 작년도에 비하여 근 배증하였으며, 흑백 분규의 악화, 미군내 기율의 이완등 제 현상에 비추어 볼때 이러한 추세는 계속될 것으로 보임.

가. 한.미 관계에 미칠 악영향

이러한 사건의 재발은 앞으로도 인종문제와 결부되어 보도되므로써 미 의회내의 소위 Black Caucus 를 자극하여 미국의 대한정책에 대한 불리한 압력으로 나타날 것이며, 특히 해외주재 미군의 철수를 요구하는 미국내 여론이 고조되고있는 현 시점에서 한.미관계 전반에 걸쳐 좋지않은 영향을 미칠 우려가 있음.

나. 기지 주변 주민의 피해

한.미간의 충돌사건이 미국내에서 정치문제화되고 있는 경향에 비추어 주한미군 당국은 사건의 예방을 위하여 강경 조치를 불사하고 있는바, 사건발생 지역에 대한 미군의 출입금지령등은 기지주변 주민의 생계를 위협하고 있음.

4. 대 책

가. 한국정부 조치

(1) 주미 각 공관장에게 훈령, 실정을 해명케 함.

(2) 주미대사관 공보관 해명서한 기재

Washington Post (7. 17.자)
Evening Star (7. 20.자)

(3) 8. 18. 외무부 주관하에 내무, 법무, 보사, 서울시, 관광협회등 실무자 회의를 개최하여 사건 방지책 협의

30

(4) 8. 31. 본직은 이에 관련된 문제점, 대책등에
대하여 국무회의에 보고하고, 곧 군,민관계 임시
분과위를 합동위원회 산하에 구성할 계획을 설명
하고 관계부처의 협조를 요청함.

(5) 9. 1. 본직은 주한미 Underhill 공사의
방문을 받고 앞으로 대책을 협의함.

(6) 9.3. 주미 각 공관장에게 이 문제의 진전을 통보하고
현지에서 홍보하도록 지시함.

나. 주한 미군 당국의조치

(1) 대민관계 개선에 관한 정책지시 하달 (7. 15.).

(2) 평택 안정리 미군 외출 금지 (7. 12. - 8.30.)
(한국 업자들에게 흑백 차별대우 금지, 위생시설의
개선, 성병 퇴치를 위한 조치등을 출입금지 해제
조건으로 제시함.)

(3) 이태원 접객업자들을 조치하여 인종 차별을 않겠다는
서약서에 서명케 함. (8. 6.)

(4) 동두천 독거리 출입 금지 (8. 18.)

(5) 로저스 미 국무장관 전 재외공관장에게 인종 차별
문제에 직접 개입하여 해소에 노력하라고 지시함.
(8. 27.)

다. 한.미 합동 조치

(1) 한.미 합동위에서 본건을 상정, 대책을 협의 (7. 29.)

(2) 군,민관계 임시분과위원회 설치 합의(9. 2.)

그간 외무부에서는 한.미 합동위를 통하여
미측과 대책을 협의하여 왔으나, 문제의 근본적
해결을 위하여는 기지주변지역에서 뿐만 아니라

중앙에서도 한.미간의 긴밀한 협력이 필요하며,
또한 정부관계 부처의 공동노력이 필수적인바,
이 목적을 위하여 군,민관계 분과위 (ad hoc Subcommittee for Civil-Military Relations)
를 설치하기로 합의 하였음.

(가) 분과위의 구성

동 분과위의 운용을 통하여 소기의 성과를 거두기 위하여 외무부, 법무부, 내무부, 교통부, 보사부의 관계관을 한국측 위원으로 위촉하기로 하였음.

(나) 분과위의 기능

동 분과위에서는 주한미군과 기지주변 주민간의 문제뿐만 아니라 미군부대에 근무하는 한국인 종업원과 미군간의 제 문제등의 실태를 조사, 파악하고 미군과 한국 민간인간에 발생하는 모든 문제의 해결책을 합동위에 건의하는 임무를 수행하게 될 것임.

참고 자료

1. 미국내의 반향

가. 평택사건에 대한 AP 보도 (7. 10.)를 미국신문들이 게재

나. 미 하원 외무위 Executive Session 에서 흑인의원들이 한국인의 인종 차별 비난 발언 (7. 14.)

다. Dellums 하원의원 담화 발표 (7. 15.)

라. Mitchell 하원의원의 비난 발표 (7. 19. Boltimore Sun)

마. 미 하원 흑인출신 의원 12명이 닉슨 대통령에게 대책을 촉구하는

32

연판장을 보냄 (7. 22.)

2. 주한 미군 범죄 통계

1970년 480 건

1971년 상반기 467 건

3. 관광 유양업소 현황

전 국 총 214 개소

평택지역	(71. 6. 30. 현재)	(70. 6. 30. 현재)
미군 총수	4, 632	5,305
한국접객업소	20	19
위안부 수	2,490	1,685

첨부 : (1) 미 의원 연판장

(2) 로저스 국무장관 지시문

(3) 분과위원회 설치 합의서. 끝

CHARLES C. DIGGS, JR.
13th District, Michigan

DISTRICT OFFICES:
1201 E. Grand Blvd. 48211
Area Code 313, 925-0300
6523 Grand River, 48208
Area Code 313, 898-1900

MISS DOROTHY QUARKER
CHIEF OF STAFF

Congress of the United States
House of Representatives
Washington, D.C. 20515

7111279

COMMITTEES:
FOREIGN AFFAIRS
SUBCOMMITTEES:
AFRICA, CHAIRMAN
ASIAN AND PACIFIC AFFAIRS
COMMITTEE ON THE DISTRICT OF COLUMBIA
AD HOC COMMITTEE:
CHAIRMAN, CONGRESSIONAL BLACK CAUCUS
WASHINGTON OFFICE:
2464 RAYBURN BUILDING
AREA CODE 202, 225-2261

July 22, 1971

The President
The White House
Washington, D. C. 20500

ACTION is assigned to

Dear Mr. President:

We are deeply disturbed with continuing racism practiced against minority servicemen stationed throughout the worl[d]. Specifically, the Congressional Black Caucus is writing t[o] express concern for failure at both the Ambassadorial and military command levels to carry out any policy aiming to achieve equitable treatment of minority servicemen.

On the heels of reports detailing irregularities in military justice and discriminatory housing practices in Germany, we are now treated to accounts of "benign neglect" erupting into violence in South Korea. The recent incidents in South Korea is not an aberration. Conditions similar to those in South Korea are now occurring at the majority of overseas military installations where minority servicemen are stationed.

On May 18, 1971, you rejected our recommendation for the establishment of a Civil Rights Division within the Department of Defense with sufficient funding and personnel for the handling of racial discrimination complaints. We were advised at that time thatthe "commitment of all supervisory and command personnel" offered the preferable route to resolution of the black GI's grievances. Since it is inconceivable that a mandate of the Commander-In-Chief did not reach Camp Humphreys, Korea, we are forced to conclude that a serious gap continues to exist between Administration policy statements and the requirements imposed upon overseas commanders.

The recent violence in South Korea was preceded by signs which only the most insensitive and uncommitted could ignore. A day long sit-in, grenade explosions at Pyongtack, South Korea, and the open existence of off-base discrimination in the area surrounding Camp Humphreys, all pointed to the need for affirmative action consistent with announced policy.

/s/ CHARLES C. DIGGS, JR. — JOHN CONYERS, JR.
SHIRLEY CHISHOLM — WALTER FAUNTROY
GEORGE COLLINS — RALPH H. METCALFE
WILLIAM CLAY — ROBERT N. C. NIX
RONALD V. DELLUMS — LOUIS STOKES
AUGUSTUS F. HAWKINS
PARREN J. MITCHELL

7-24-71
0016559

The President - 2 - July 22, 1971

The Caucus seeks an immediate report on the Administration's intent for dealing with these very serious problems.

Why did authorities at Camp Humphreys fail to comply with regulations requiring them to use alternatives ranging from negotiation to sanctions as a means of elimination of off-base discrimination? Have our commanders in certain areas of the world been quietly provided guidelines contrary to your response of May 18th?

In addition to the failures of military commanders, the neglect of our Ambassadors in these so-called Allied nations is a very real element in this crisis. When racism rears its ugly head in Germany or Korea, black Americans assigned to "protect freedom" have every right to expect, and indeed demand, the vigorous intervention of our embassies. In the face of mounting evidence that these expectations will not be met, the Congressional Black Caucus is forced to reconsider support of appropriations for the maintenance of troops in countries where the human dignity of black soldiers has been violated.

Congressional precedent was set by the House Foreign Affairs Committee on July 14, 1971, when it blocked $50 million in military aid to South Korea, among other reasons, until Korean leaders deal effectively with the abuse of minority servicemen. We strongly urge the Administration to undertake procedures to withhold all assistance until written assurance is received that positive action is being taken by host country governments to assure equitable treatment of all U.S. troops.

The Congressional Black Caucus and all minority servicemen anxiously await your response, which we trust will be forthcoming as expeditiously as possible.

Sincerely,

CHARLES C DIGGS, JR.
CHAIRMAN,
Congressional Black Caucus

SHIRLEY CHISHOLM WILLIAM L. CLAY

GEORGE COLLINS RONALD V. DELLUMS

35

AUGUSTUS F. HAWKINS WALTER FAUNTROY

PARREN J. MITCHELL RALPH H. METCALFE

CHARLES B. RANGEL ROBERT N. C. NIX

JOHN CONYERS, JR. LOUIS STOKES

cc: Hon. Melvin R. Laird, Secretary, Department of Defense
Hon. Robert C. Seamans, Jr., Secretary of the Air Force
Hon. John H. Chafee, Secretary of the Navy
Hon. Robert F. Froehlke, Secretary of the Army
Gen. Leonard F. Chapman, Jr., Commandant, U.S.M.C.
Hon. William P. Rogers, Secretary of State

36

Mr. Underhill presented to Minister Kim
71. 9. 1.

별첨2

27 AUGUST 1971

FROM: SECSTATE WASH DC

TO: ALL DIPLOMATIC AND CONSULAR POSTS

UNCLASSIFIED STATE 157549

SUBJECT: DISCRIMINATION PROBLEMS OF MINORITY US SERVICEMEN STATIONED ABROAD.

JOINT STATE/DEFENSE MESSAGE

PROBLEMS OF RACIAL DISCRIMINATION FACED BY US MINORITY SERVICEMEN SERVING OVERSEAS ARE OF SERIOUS CONCERN TO THE PRESIDENT AND THE SECRETARIES OF STATE AND DEFENSE. THE PURPOSE OF THIS MESSAGE IS TO REEMPHASIZE OUR CONTINUED INTEREST IN THE ELIMINATION OF INEQUALITIES IN THE TREATMENT OF OUR MILITARY PERSONNEL AND TO ENCOURAGE REPORTING OF MEASURES TAKEN TO THAT END.

IN HIS MESSAGE OF DECEMBER 9, 1969, THE PRESIDENT STATED THAT HE EXPECTED AMBASSADORS AND MILITARY COMMANDERS TO QUOTE MAINTAIN CLOSE RELATIONS WITH EACH OTHER, TO KEEP EACH OTHER CURRENTLY INFORMED ON MATTERS OF MUTUAL INTEREST AND IN GENERAL TO COOPERATE IN CARRYING OUT OUR NATIONAL POLICY. UNQUOTE. THE MORALE AND WELFARE OF OUR MEN AND WOMEN SERVING IN UNIFORM OVERSEAS IS A PRIORITY MATTER WITHIN THE SCOPE OF THAT INSTRUCTION. RECENT EVENTS, HOWEVER, HAVE DEMONSTRATED THE NEED FOR PARTICULAR ATTENTION TO THIS MATTER AS IT RELATES TO HOUSING AND PUBLIC ACCOMMODATIONS IN COMMUNITIES ADJACENT TO MILITARY INSTALLATIONS.

AMBASSADORS IN COUNTRIES WHERE US SERVICEMEN ARE STATIONED ARE URGED TO SCHEDULE PERIODIC MEETINGS WITH SENIOR MILITARY COMMANDERS TO DISCUSS CURRENT EFFORTS AND TO COORDINATE FUTURE PLANS FOR ELIMINATING RACIAL DISCRIMINATION AND LESSENING THE IMPACT OF CULTURAL CONFLICTS BETWEEN MILITARY PERSONNEL AND FOREIGN NATIONALS. SUCH COORDINATION SHOULD INCLUDE DISCUSSIONS WITH FOREIGN OFFICIALS DESIGNED TO ELICIT SPECIFIC COMMITMENTS REGARDING PROGRAMS TO BE IMPLEMENTED EITHER SEPARATELY OR IN CONJUNCTION WITH THE EFFORTS OF MILITARY COMMANDERS.

37

SIMILAR MEETINGS BETWEEN PRINCIPAL OFFICERS AND LOCAL COMMANDERS AT MILITARY POSTS WITHIN THEIR DISTRICT ARE ENCOURAGED.

AMBASSADORS AND PRINCIPAL OFFICERS ARE URGED TO CONTINUE TO KEEP THEMSELVES PERSONALLY INFORMED ON MATTERS CONCERNING THE STATE OF RACIAL DIFFICULTIES IN RELATIONS BETWEEN US SERVICEMEN AND FOREIGN NATIONALS WITHIN THEIR AREAS OF CONCERN. IN ADDITION TO ALTERNATIVES CURRENTLY EMBODIED IN MILITARY REGULATIONS, ADDRESSEES ARE REQUESTED TO SUGGEST METHODS FOR IMPROVING THE COOPERATION OF HOST GOVERNMENTS IN THIS MATTER.

BECAUSE OF THE SERIOUSNESS OF THIS PROBLEM AND THE POTENTIAL IT HAS FOR DAMAGING THE EFFECTIVENESS OF OUR MILITARY FORCES, POSTS WITH SIGNIFICANT NUMBERS OF MILITARY PERSONNEL WITHIN THEIR AREA ARE REQUESTED TO INFORM THE DEPARTMENT OF MEASURES THEY HAVE TAKEN IN RESPONSE TO THIS MESSAGE AS SOON AS POSSIBLE.

ROGERS

38

공 란

May 27, 1971
NUMBER 5500.11

ASD (M&RA)

Department of Defense Directive

SUBJECT Nondiscrimination in Federally Assisted Programs

Ref: Public Law 88-352, "The Civil Rights Act of 1964," 78 Stat. 241, July 2, 1964

I. PURPOSE

The purpose of this Directive is to effectuate the provisions of Title VI of the Civil Rights Act of 1964 (hereafter referred to as the "Act") to the end that no person in the United States shall, on the ground of race, color, or national origin, be excluded from participation in, be denied the benefits of, or be otherwise subjected to discrimination under any program or activity receiving Federal financial assistance from any component of the Department of Defense.

II. DEFINITIONS

A. "Component" means the Office of the Secretary of Defense, a military department or a Defense agency.

B. "Responsible Department official" means the Secretary of Defense or other official of the Department of Defense or component thereof who by law or by delegation has the principal responsibility within the Department or component for the administration of the law extending such assistance.

C. The term "United States" means the States of the United States, the District of Columbia, Puerto Rico, the Virgin Islands, American Samoa, Guam, Wake Island, the Canal Zone, and the territories and possessions of the United States, and the term "State" means any one of the foregoing.

40

D. The term "Federal financial assistance" includes (1) grants and loans of Federal funds, (2) the grant or donation of Federal property and interests in property, (3) the detail of Federal personnel, (4) the sale and lease of, and the permission to use (on other than a casual or transient basis), Federal property or any interest in such property without consideration or at a nominal consideration, or at a consideration which is reduced for the purpose of assisting the recipient, or in recognition of the public interest to be served by such sale or lease to the recipient, and (5) any Federal agreement, arrangement, or other contract which has as one of its purposes the provision of assistance.

E. The term "program" includes any program, project, or activity for the provision of services, financial aid, or other benefits to individuals, or for the provision of facilities for furnishing services, financial aid or other benefits to individuals. The services, financial aid, or other benefits provided under a program receiving Federal financial assistance shall be deemed to include any services, financial aid, or other benefits provided with the aid of Federal financial assistance or with the aid of any non-Federal funds, property, or other resources required to be expended or made available for the program to meet matching requirements or other conditions which must be met in order to receive the Federal financial assistance, and to include any services, financial aid, or other benefits provided in or through a facility provided with the aid of Federal financial assistance or such non-Federal resources.

F. The term "facility" includes all or any portion of structures, equipment, or other real or personal property or interests therein, and the provision of facilities includes the construction, expansion, renovation, remodeling, alteration or acquisition of facilities.

G. The term "recipient" means any State, political subdivision of any State, or instrumentality of any State or political subdivision, any public or private agency, institution, or organization, or other entity, or any individual, in any State, to whom Federal financial assistance is extended, directly or through another recipient, for any program, including any successor, assign, or transferee thereof, but such term does not include any ultimate beneficiary under any such program.

H. The term "primary recipient" means any recipient which is authorized or required to extend Federal financial assistance to another recipient for the purpose of carrying out a program.

I. The term "applicant" means one who submits an application, request, or plan required to be approved by a responsible Department official, or by a primary recipient, as a condition to eligibility for Federal financial assistance, and the term "application" means such an application, request or plan.

III. APPLICATION

This Directive applies to any program for which Federal financial assistance is authorized under a law administered by any component of the Department of Defense, including the Federally-assisted programs and activities listed in Appendix A of this Directive. It applies to money paid, property transferred, or other Federal financial assistance extended under any such program after the effective date of this Directive pursuant to approval prior to such effective date. This Directive does not apply to (a) any Federal financial assistance by way of insurance guaranty contracts, (b) money paid, property transferred, or other assistance extended under any such program before the effective date of this Directive, (c) any assistance to any individual who is the ultimate beneficiary under any such program, or (d) any employment practice, under any such program, of any employer, employment agency, or labor organization, except as noted in Subsection IV.B.4., below. The fact that a program or activity is not listed in Appendix A shall not mean, if Title VI of the Act is otherwise applicable, that such program is not covered. Other programs under statutes now in force or hereinafter enacted may be added to this list by notice published in the Federal Register.

IV. POLICY

A. General. No person in the United States shall, on the ground of race, color, or national origin be excluded from participation in, be denied the benefits of, or be otherwise subjected to discrimination under any program to which this Directive applies.

B. Specific Discriminatory Actions Prohibited.

1. A recipient under any program to which this Directive applies may not, directly or through contractual or other arrangements, on the ground of race, color, or national origin:

a. Deny an individual any service, financial aid, or other benefit provided under the program;

b. Provide any service, financial aid, or other benefit to an individual which is different, or is provided in a different manner, from that provided to others under the program;

c. In determining the site or location of facilities, make selections with the purpose of excluding individuals from, denying them the benefits of, or subjecting them to discrimination under any program to which this Directive applies, on the grounds of race, color, or national origin; or with the purpose or effect of defeating or substantially impairing the accomplishment of the objectives of the Act or this Directive;

d. Subject an individual to segregation or separate treatment in any matter related to his receipt of any service, financial aid, or other benefit under the program;

e. Restrict an individual in any way in the enjoyment of any advantage or privilege enjoyed by others receiving any service, financial aid, or other benefit under the program;

f. Treat an individual differently from others in determining whether he satisfies any admission, enrollment, quota, eligibility, membership or other requirement or condition which individuals must meet in order to be provided any service, financial aid, or other benefit provided under the program;

g. Be prohibited from considering race, color or national origin if the purpose and effect are to remove or overcome the consequences of practices or impediments which have restricted the availability of, or participation in, the program or activity receiving Federal financial assistance, on the grounds of race, color or national origin. Where previous discriminatory practice or usage tends, on the grounds of race, color or national origin, to exclude individuals from participation in, to deny them the benefits of, or to subject them to discrimination under any program or activity to which this Directive applies the applicant or recipient has an obligation to take reasonable action to remove or overcome the consequences of the prior discriminatory practice or usage, and to accomplish the purposes of the Act;

h. Deny an individual an opportunity to participate in the program through the provision of services or otherwise or afford him an opportunity to do so which is different from that afforded others under the program.

2. A recipient, in determining the types of services, financial aid, or other benefits, or facilities which will be provided under any such program, or the class of individuals to whom, or the situations in which, such services, financial aid, other benefits, or facilities will be provided under any such program, or the class of individuals to be afforded an opportunity to participate in any such program, may not, directly or through contractual or other arrangements, utilize criteria or methods of administration which have the effect of subjecting individuals to discrimination because of their race, color, or national origin, or have the effect of defeating or substantially impairing accomplishment of the objectives of the program with respect to individuals of a particular race, color, or national origin.

3. As used in this Section the services, financial aid, or other benefits provided under a program receiving Federal financial assistance shall be deemed to include any service, financial aid, or other benefit provided in or through a facility provided with the aid of Federal financial assistance.

4. Where a primary objective of the Federal financial assistance is not to provide employment, but nevertheless discrimination on the grounds of race, color or national origin in the employment practices of the recipient or other persons subject to this Directive tends, on the grounds of race, color or national origin of the intended beneficiaries, to exclude intended beneficiaries from participation in, to deny them the benefits of, or to subject them to discrimination under any program to which this directive applies, the recipient or other persons subject to this Directive are prohibited from (directly or through contractual or other arrangements) subjecting an individual to discrimination on the grounds of race, color, or national origin in its employment, practices under such program (including recruitment or recruitment advertising;

employment, [illegible]off or termination; upgrading, [illegible]motion or transfer; rates of pay or other forms of compensation; and use of facilities), to the extent necessary to assure equality of opportunity to, and nondiscriminatory treatment of the beneficiaries.

5. The enumeration of specific forms of prohibited discrimination in this Subsection does not limit the generality of the prohibition in Subsection IV.A. of this Section.

V. RESPONSIBILITIES

A. The Assistant Secretary of Defense (Manpower and Reserve Affairs) shall be responsible for insuring that the policies of this Directive are effectuated throughout the Department of Defense. He may review from time to time as he deems necessary the implementation of these policies by the components of the Department of Defense.

B. The Secretary of each Military Department is responsible for implementing this Directive with respect to programs and activities receiving financial assistance from his Military Department; and the Assistant Secretary of Defense (Manpower and Reserve Affairs) is responsible for similarly implementing this Directive with respect to all other components of the Department of Defense. Each may designate official(s) to fulfill this responsibility in accordance with Subsection II. B. of this Directive.

C. The Assistant Secretary of Defense (Manpower and Reserve Affairs) or, after consultation with the Assistant Secretary of Defense (Manpower and Reserve Affairs), the Secretary of each Military Department or other responsible Department official designated by the Assistant Secretary of Defense (Manpower and Reserve Affairs) may assign to officials of other departments or agencies of the Government, with the consent of such departments or agencies, responsibilities in connection with the effectuation of the purposes of Title VI of the Act and this Directive (other than responsibility for final decision as provided in Section XI.), including the achievement of effective coordination and maximum uniformity within the Department and within the Executive Branch of the Government in the application of Title VI and this Directive to similar programs and in similar situations.

Any action taken, determination made, or requirement imposed by an official of another Department or Agency acting pursuant to an assignment of responsibility under this subsection shall have the same effect as though such action had been taken by the responsible official of this agency.

VI. ASSURANCES REQUIRED

A. General

1. Every application for Federal financial assistance to carry out a program to which this Directive applies, except a program to which Subsection VI.B. applies and every application for Federal financial assistance to provide a facility shall as a condition to its approval and the extension of any Federal financial assistance pursuant to the application, contain or be accompanied by an assurance that the program will be conducted or the facility operated in compliance with all requirements imposed by or pursuant to this Directive.

In the case where the Federal financial assistance is to provide or is in the form of personal property, or real property or interest therein or structures thereon, the assurance shall obligate the recipient, or, in the case of a subsequent transfer, the transferee, for the period during which the property or structures are used for a purpose for which the Federal financial assistance is extended or for another purpose involving the provision of similar services and benefits, or for as long as the recipient retains ownership or possession of the property, whichever is longer. In all other cases the assurance shall obligate the recipient for the period during which Federal financial assistance is extended pursuant to the application. In any case in which Federal financial assistance is extended without an application having been made, such extension shall be subject to the same assurances as if an application had been made. The responsible Department official shall specify the form of the foregoing assurances for each program, and the extent to which like assurances will be required of subgrantees, contractors and subcontractors, transferees, successors in interest, and other participants in the program. Any such assurance shall include provisions which give the United States a right to seek its judicial enforcement.

2. In the case of real property, structures or improvements thereon, or interests therein, which was acquired through a program of Federal financial assistance, or in the case where Federal financial assistance is provided in the form of a transfer of real property or interest therein from the Federal Government, the instrument effecting or recording the transfer, shall contain a covenant running with the land assuring nondiscrimination for the period during which the real property is used for a purpose for which the Federal financial assistance is extended or for another purpose involving the provision of similar services or benefits, or for as long as the recipient retains ownership or possession of the property, whichever is longer. Where no transfer of property is involved, but property is improved under a program of Federal financial assistance, the recipient shall agree to include such a covenant in any subsequent transfer of such property. Where the property is obtained from the Federal government, such covenant may also include a condition coupled with a right to be reserved by the Department to revert title to the property in the event of a breach of the covenant where, in the discretion of the responsible Department official, such a condition and right of reverter is appropriate to the program under which the real property is obtained and to the nature of the grant and the grantee. In the event a transferee of real property proposes to mortgage or otherwise encumber the real property as security for financing construction of new, or improvement of existing facilities on such property for the purposes for which the property was transferred, the responsible Department official may agree, upon request of the transferee and if necessary to accomplish such financing, and upon such conditions as he deems appropriate, to forbear the exercise of such right to revert title for so long as the lien of such mortgage or other encumbrance remains effective. In programs receiving Federal financial assistance in the form, or for the acquisition of real property or an interest in real property, to the extent that rights to space on, over, or under any such property are included as part of the program receiving such assistance, the nondiscrimination requirements of this Directive shall extend to any facility located wholly or in part in such space.

3. The assurance required in the case of a transfer of surplus personal property shall be inserted in a written agreement

by and between the Department of Defense component concerned and the recipient.

B. Continuing State Programs. Every application by a State or a State agency to carry out a program involving continuing Federal financial assistance to which this Directive applies shall as a condition to its approval and the extension of any Federal financial assistance pursuant to the application (1) contain or be accompanied by a statement that the program is (or, in the case of a new program, will be) conducted in compliance with all requirements imposed by or pursuant to this Directive, and (2) provide or be accompanied by provision for such methods of administration for the program as are found by the responsible Department official to give reasonable assurance that the applicant and all recipients of Federal financial assistance under such program will comply with all requirements imposed by or pursuant to this Directive. In cases of continuing State programs in which applications are not made, the extension of Federal financial assistance shall be subject to the same conditions under this Subsection as if applications had been made.

C. Assurances from Institutions

1. In the case of Federal financial assistance to an institution of higher education, the assurance required by this Section shall extend to admission practices and to all other practices relating to the treatment of students.

2. The assurance required with respect to an institution of higher education, or any other institution, insofar as the assurance relates to the institution's practices with respect to admission or other treatment of individuals as students of the institution or to the opportunity to participate in the provision of services or other benefits to such individuals, shall be applicable to the entire institution unless the applicant establishes, to the satisfaction of the responsible Department official, that the institution's practices in designated parts or programs of the institution will in no way affect its practices in the program of the institution for which Federal financial assistance is sought, or the beneficiaries of or participants in such program. If in any such case the assistance sought is for the construction of a

facility or part of a facility, the assurance shall in any event extend to the entire facility and to facilities operated in connection therewith.

D. Elementary and Secondary Schools. The requirement of Subsection VI.A., B., or C., above, with respect to any elementary or secondary school or school system shall be deemed to be satisfied if such school or school system (1) is subject to a final order of a court of the United States for the desegregation of such school or school system, and provides an assurance that it will comply with such order, including any future modification of such order, or (2) submits a plan for the desegregation of such school or school system which the responsible official of the Department of Health, Education and Welfare determines is adequate to accomplish the purposes of the Act and this Directive, and provides reasonable assurance that it will carry out such plan; in any case of continuing Federal financial assistance the said Department officer may reserve the right to redetermine, after such period as may be specified by him, the adequacy of the plan to accomplish the purpose of the Act or this Directive within the earliest practicable time. In any case in which a final order of a court of the United States for the desegregation of such school or school system is entered after submission of such a plan, such plan shall be revised to conform to such final order, including any future modification of said order.

VII. COMPLIANCE INFORMATION

A. Cooperation and Assistance. Each responsible Department official shall to the fullest extent practicable seek the cooperation of recipients in obtaining compliance with this Directive and shall provide assistance and guidance to recipients to help them comply voluntarily with this Directive.

B. Compliance Reports. Each recipient shall keep such records and submit to the responsible Department official timely, complete and accurate compliance reports at such times, and in such form and containing such information, as the responsible Department official may determine to be necessary to enable him to ascertain whether the recipient has complied or is complying with this Directive. In the case of any program under which a primary recipient extends Federal financial assistance to any other recipient, such other recipient shall also submit such compliance reports to the primary recipient as may be necessary to enable the primary recipient to carry out its obligations imposed pursuant to this Directive.

C. Access to Sources of Information. Each recipient shall permit access by the responsible Department official during normal business hours to such of its books, records, accounts, and other sources of information, and its facilities as may be pertinent to ascertain compliance with this Directive. Where any information required of a recipient is in the exclusive possession of any other institution or person and this institution or person shall fail or refuse to furnish this information, the recipient shall so certify in its report and shall set forth what efforts it has made to obtain the information.

D. Information to Beneficiaries and Participants. Each recipient shall make available to participants, beneficiaries, and other interested persons such information regarding the provisions of this Directive and its applicability to the program under which the recipient receives Federal financial assistance, and make such information available to them in such manner, as the responsible Department official finds necessary to apprise such persons of the protections against discrimination assured them by the Act and this Directive.

VIII. CONDUCT OF INVESTIGATIONS

A. Periodic Compliance Reviews. The responsible Department official or his designee(s) shall from time to time review the practices of recipients to determine whether they are complying with this Directive.

B. Complaints. Any person who believes himself or any specific class of individuals to be subjected to discrimination prohibited by this Directive may by himself or by a representative file with the responsible Department official a written complaint. A complaint must be filed not later than 90 days from the date of the alleged discrimination, unless the time for filing is extended by the responsible Department official.

C. Investigations. The responsible Department official will make a prompt investigation whenever a compliance review, report, complaint, or any other information indicates a possible failure to comply with this Directive. The investigation should include, where appropriate, a review of the pertinent practices and policies of the recipient, the circumstances under which the possible non-compliance with this Directive occurred, and other

factors relevant to a determination of whether the recipient has failed to comply with this Directive.

D. Resolution of Matters

1. If an investigation pursuant to Subsection VIII. C. indicates a failure to comply with this Directive, the responsible Department official will so inform the recipient and the matter will be resolved by informal means whenever possible. If it has been determined that the matter cannot be resolved by informal means, action will be taken as provided in Section IX. of this Directive.

2. If an investigation does not warrant action pursuant to Subsection VIII. D. 1., the responsible Department official will so inform the recipient and the complainant, if any, in writing.

E. Intimidatory or Retaliatory Acts Prohibited. No recipient or other person shall intimidate, threaten, coerce, or discriminate against any individual for the purpose of interfering with any right or privilege secured by section 601 of the Act or this Directive, or because he has made a complaint, testified, assisted, or participated in any manner in an investigation, proceeding, or hearing under this Directive. The identity of complainants shall not be disclosed except when necessary to carry out the purposes of this Directive, including the conduct of any investigation, hearing or judicial proceeding arising thereunder.

IX. PROCEDURE FOR EFFECTING COMPLIANCE

A. General. If there appears to be a failure or threatened failure to comply with this Directive, and if the noncompliance or threatened noncompliance cannot be corrected by informal means, compliance with this Directive may be effected by the suspension or termination of or refusal to grant or to continue Federal financial assistance or by any other means authorized by law as determined by the responsible Department official. Such other means may include, but are not limited to (1) a reference to the Department of Justice with a recommendation that appropriate proceedings be brought to enforce any rights of the United States under any law of the United States

12

51

(including other titles of the Act), or any assurance or other contractual undertaking, and (2) any applicable proceedings under State or local law.

B. Noncompliance with Section VI. If an applicant fails or refuses to furnish an assurance required under Section VI or otherwise fails or refuses to comply with a requirement imposed by or pursuant to that section, Federal financial assistance may be refused in accordance with the procedures of paragraph C. of this Section. The component of the Department of Defense concerned shall not be required to provide assistance in such a case during the pendency of the administrative proceedings under such paragraph except that the component shall continue assistance during the pendency of such proceedings where such assistance is due and payable pursuant to an application therefor approved prior to the effective date of this Directive.

C. Termination of or Refusal to Grant or to Continue Federal Financial Assistance. Except as provided in Subsection IX. B. no order suspending, terminating or refusing to grant or continue Federal financial assistance shall become effective until (1) the responsible Department official has advised the applicant or recipient of his failure to comply and has determined that compliance cannot be secured by voluntary means; (2) there has been an express finding, after opportunity for a hearing (as provided in Section X. of this Directive), of a failure by the applicant or recipient to comply with a requirement imposed by or pursuant to this Directive; (3) the action has been approved by the Secretary of Defense pursuant to Section XI. of this Directive; and (4) the expiration of 30 days after the Secretary of Defense has filed with the committee of the House and the committee of the Senate having legislative jurisdiction over the program involved, a full written report of the circumstances and the grounds for such action. Any action to suspend or terminate or to refuse to grant or to continue Federal financial assistance shall be limited to the particular political entity, or part thereof, or other applicant or recipient as to whom such a finding has been made and shall be limited in its effect to the particular program, or part thereof, in which such noncompliance has been so found.

D. Other Means Authorized by Law. No action to affect compliance by any other means authorized by law shall be taken until (1) the

responsible Department official has determined that compliance cannot be secured by voluntary means, (2) the action has been approved by the Assistant Secretary of Defense (Manpower and Reserve Affairs), (3) the recipient or other person has been notified of its failure to comply and of the action to be taken to effect compliance, and (4) the expiration of at least 10 days from the mailing of such notice to the recipient or other person. During this period of at least 10 days additional efforts shall be made to persuade the recipient or other person to comply with this Directive and to take such corrective action as may be appropriate.

X. HEARINGS

A. Opportunity for Hearing. Whenever an opportunity for a hearing is required by Section IX. of this Directive, reasonable notice shall be given by registered or certified mail, return receipt requested, to the affected applicant or recipient. This notice shall advise the applicant or recipient of the action proposed to be taken, the specific provision under which the proposed action against it is to be taken, and the matters of fact or law asserted as the basis for this action, and either (1) fix a date not less than 20 days after the date of such notice within which the applicant or recipient may request of the responsible Department official that the matter be scheduled for hearing, or (2) advise the applicant or recipient that the matter in question has been set down for hearing at a stated place and time. The time and place so fixed shall be reasonable and shall be subject to change for cause. The complainant, if any, shall be advised of the time and place of hearing. An applicant or recipient may waive a hearing and submit written information and argument. The failure of an applicant or recipient to request a hearing under this paragraph or to appear at a hearing for which a date has been set shall be deemed to be a waiver of the right to a hearing under Section 602 of the Act and Section IX. C. of this Directive and consent to the making of a decision on the basis of such information as is available.

B. Time and Place of Hearing. Hearings shall be held at the offices of the responsible component of the Department of Defense in Washington, D. C. at a time fixed by the responsible Department official unless he determines that the convenience of the applicant or recipient or of the component requires that another place be selected. Hearings shall be held before the responsible Department official or, at his discretion, before a hearing examiner designated by him.

C. Hearing Examiner. The examiner shall be a field grade officer or civilian employee above the grade of GS-12 (or the equivalent) who shall be a person admitted to practice law before a Federal court or the highest court of a State.

D. Right to Counsel. In all proceedings under this Section, the applicant or recipient and the responsible component of the Department shall have the right to be represented by counsel.

E. Procedures

1. The recipient shall receive an open hearing at which he or his counsel may examine any witnesses present. Both the responsible Department official and the applicant or recipient shall be entitled to introduce all relevant evidence on the issues as stated in the notice for hearing or as determined by the officer conducting the hearing at the outset of or during the hearing.

2. Technical rules of evidence shall not apply to hearings conducted pursuant to this Directive, but rules or principles designed to assure production of the most credible evidence available and to subject testimony to test by cross-examination shall be applied where reasonably necessary by the officer conducting the hearing. The hearing officer may exclude irrelevant, immaterial, or unduly repetitious evidence. All documents and other evidence offered or taken for record shall be open to examination by the parties and opportunity shall be given to refute facts and arguments advanced on either side of the issues. A transcript shall be made of the oral evidence except to the extent the substance thereof is stipulated for the record. All decisions shall be based upon the hearing record and written findings shall be made.

F. Consolidated or Joint Hearings. In cases in which the same or related facts are asserted to constitute noncompliance with this Directive with respect to two or more programs to which this Directive applies, or noncompliance with this Directive and the regulations of one or more other Federal departments or agencies issued under Title VI of the Act, the Assistant Secretary of

Defense (Manpower and Reserve Affairs), the Secretary of a Military Department, or other responsible Department official designated by the Assistant Secretary of Defense (Manpower and Reserve Affairs) after consultation with the Assistant Secretary of Defense (Manpower and Reserve Affairs) may, by agreement with such other departments or agencies where applicable, provide for the conduct of consolidated or joint hearings, and for the application to such hearings of appropriate procedures not inconsistent with this Directive. Final decisions in such cases, insofar as this Directive is concerned, shall be made in accordance with Section XI.

XI. DECISIONS AND NOTICES

A. Decision by Person Other Than the Responsible Department Official. If the hearing is held by a hearing examiner such hearing examiner shall either make an initial decision, if so authorized, or certify the entire record including his recommended findings and proposed decision to the responsible Department official for a final decision, and a copy of such initial decision or certification shall be mailed to the applicant or recipient. Where the initial decision is made by the hearing examiner the applicant or recipient may within 30 days of the mailing of such notice of initial decision file with the responsible Department official his exceptions to the initial decision, with his reasons therefor. In the absence of exceptions, the responsible Department official may on his own motion within 45 days after the initial decision serve on the applicant or recipient a notice that he will review the decision. Upon the filing of such exceptions or of such notice of review the responsible Department official shall review the initial decision and issue his own decision thereon including the reasons therefor. In the absence of either exceptions or a notice of review the initial decision shall constitute the final decision of the responsible Department official.

B. Decisions on Record or Review by the Responsible Department Official. Whenever a record is certified to the responsible Department official for decision or he reviews the decision of a hearing examiner pursuant to Section XI.A. or whenever the responsible Department official conducts the hearing, the applicant or recipient shall be given reasonable opportunity to file with him briefs or other written statements of its contentions, and a copy of the final decision of the responsible Department official shall be given in writing to the applicant or recipient and to the complainant, if any.

C. Decisions on Record Where a Hearing is Waived. Whenever a hearing is waived pursuant to Section X. A. a decision shall be made by the responsible Department official on the record and a copy of such decision shall be given in writing to the applicant or recipient, and to the complainant, if any.

D. Rulings Required. Each decision of a hearing officer or responsible Department official shall set forth his ruling on each finding, conclusion, or exception presented, and shall identify the requirement or requirements imposed by or pursuant to this Directive with which it is found that the applicant or recipient has failed to comply.

E. Approval by the Secretary of Defense. Any final decision of a responsible Department official which provides for the suspension or termination of, or the refusal to grant or continue Federal financial assistance, or the imposition of any other sanction available under this Directive or the Act, shall promptly be transmitted to the Secretary of Defense, who may approve such decision, may vacate it, or remit or mitigate any sanction imposed.

F. Contents of Orders. The final decision may provide for suspension or termination of, or refusal to grant or continue Federal financial assistance, in whole or in part, under the program involved, and may contain such terms, conditions, and other provisions as are consistent with and will effectuate the purposes of the Act and this Directive, including provisions designed to assure that no Federal financial assistance will thereafter be extended under such program to the applicant or recipient determined by such decision to be in default in its performance of an assurance given by it pursuant to this Directive, or to have otherwise failed to comply with this Directive, unless and until it corrects its noncompliance and satisfies the responsible Department official that it will fully comply with this Directive.

G. Post-termination Proceedings

1. An applicant or recipient adversely affected by an order issued under Subsection XI. F. shall be restored to full eligibility to receive Federal financial assistance if it satisfies the terms and conditions of that order for such eligibility or if it brings itself into compliance with this Directive and provides reasonable assurance that it will fully comply with this Directive.

2. Any applicant or recipient adversely affected by an order entered pursuant to Subsection XI. F. above may at any time request the responsible Department official to restore fully its eligibility to receive Federal financial assistance. Any such request shall be supported by information showing that the applicant or recipient has met the requirements of Subsection XI. G. 1. above. If the responsible Department official determines that those requirements have been satisfied, he shall restore such eligibility.

3. If the responsible Department official denies any such request, the applicant or recipient may submit a request for a hearing in writing, specifying why it believes such official to have been in error. It shall thereupon be given an expeditious hearing, with a decision on the record, in accordance with rules of procedure issued by the responsible Department official. The applicant or recipient will be restored to such eligibility if it proves at such a hearing that it satisfied the requirements of Subsection XI. G. 1., above. While proceedings under this Subsection are pending, the sanctions imposed by the order issued under Subsection XI. F. shall remain in effect.

XII. JUDICIAL REVIEW

Action taken pursuant to Section 602 of the Act is subject to judicial review as provided in Section 603 of the Act.

XIII. EFFECT ON OTHER ISSUANCES

All issuances heretofore issued by any officer of the Department of Defense or its components which impose requirements designed to prohibit any discrimination against individuals on the ground of race, color, or national origin under any program to which this Directive applies, and which authorize the suspension or termination of or refusal to grant or to continue Federal financial assistance to any applicant for or recipient of such assistance under such program for failure to comply with such requirements, are hereby superseded to the extent that such discrimination is prohibited by this Directive, except that nothing in this Directive shall be deemed to relieve any person of any obligation assumed or imposed under any such superseded regulation, order, instruction, or like direction prior to the effective date of this Directive.

Nothing in this Directive, however, shall be deemed to supersede any of the following (including future amendments thereof): (1) Executive Orders 10925, 11114, and 11246 and issuances thereunder, (2) the "Standards for a Merit System of Personnel Administration," issued jointly by the Secretaries of Defense, of Health, Education and Welfare, and of Labor, 28 F. R. 734, or (3) Executive Order 11063 and issuances thereunder, or any other issuances, insofar as such Order or issuances prohibit discrimination on the ground of race, color, or national origin in any program or situation to which this Directive is inapplicable, or prohibit discrimination on any other ground.

XIV. IMPLEMENTATION

The Secretary of each Military Department shall submit regulations implementing this Directive to the Assistant Secretary of Defense (Manpower and Reserve Affairs).

XV. EFFECTIVE DATE AND CANCELLATION

This Directive shall become effective on the 30th day following the date of its publication in the Federal Register. DoD Directive 5500.11, December 28, 1964 is superseded and cancelled.

Deputy Secretary of Defense

Enclosure - 1
Appendix A

58

APPENDIX A

FEDERAL FINANCIAL ASSISTANCE TO WHICH THIS DIRECTIVE APPLIES

1. The Army and Air National Guard (Title 32, United States Code).

2. Various programs involving loan or other disposition of surplus property (various general and specialized statutory provisions including: 40 United States Code 483, 484, 512; 49 United States Code 1101 - 1119; 10 United States Code 2541, 2542, 2543, 2572, 2662, 7308, 7541, 7542, 7545, 7546, 7547).

3. National Program for Promotion of Rifle Practice (10 United States Code 4307 and annual Department of Defense Appropriation Act).

4. National Defense Cadet Corps Program (10 United States Code 3540(b), 4651).

5. Office of Civil Defense assistance to programs of adult education in civil defense subjects (50 United States Code App. 2281 (e), (f)).

6. Office of Civil Defense radiological instruments grants (50 United States Code App. 2281 (h).

7. Office of Civil Defense program (with Public Health Service) for development of instructional materials on medical self-help (50 United States Code App. 2281 (e), (f)).

8. Office of Civil Defense university extension programs for civil defense instructor training (50 United States Code App. 2281 (e)).

9. Office of Civil Defense programs for survival supplies and equipment, survival training, emergency operating center construction, and personnel and administrative expenses (50 United States Code App. 2281 (i), 2285).

10. Office of Civil Defense Shelter Provisioning Program (50 United States Code App. 2281 (h)).

11. Office of Civil Defense assistance to students attending Office of Civil Defense schools (50 United States Code App. 2281 (e)).

59

12. Office of Civil Defense loans of equipment or materials from OCD stockpiles for civil defense, including local disaster purposes (50 United States Code App. 2281).

13. Navy Science Cruiser Program (Sec Nav Instruction 5720.19A).

14. Civil Air Patrol (10 United States Code 9441).

15. Research grants made under the authority of Public Law 85-934 (42 USC 1892).

16. Contracts with nonprofit institutions of higher education or with non-profit organizations whose primary purpose is the conduct of scientific research, wherein title to equipment purchased with funds under such contracts may be vested in such institutions or organizations under the authority of Public Law 85-934 (42 USC 1891).

17. Army Corps of Engineers participation in cooperative investigations and studies concerning erosion of shores of coastal and lake waters (33 United States Code 426).

18. Army Corps of Engineers assistance in the construction of works for the restoration and protection of shores and beaches (33 United States Code 426 e-h).

19. Public park and recreational facilities at water resource development projects under the administrative jurisdiction of the Department of the Army (16 United States Code 460d and Federal Water Project Recreation Act, Public Law 89-72, 79 Stat. 218, July 9, 1965).

20. Payment to States of proceeds of lands acquired by the United States for flood control, navigation, and allied purposes (33 United States Code 701-c-3).

21. Grants of easements without consideration, or at a nominal or reduced consideration, on lands under the control of the Department of the Army at water resource development projects. (33 United States Code 558c and 702 d-1; 10 United States Code 2668 and 2669; 43 United States Code 961; 40 United States Code 319).

22. Army Corps of Engineers assistance in the construction of small boat harbor projects (33 United States Code 540 and 577, and 47 Stat. 42, February 10, 1932).

23. Emergency bank protection works constructed by the Army Corps of Engineers for protection of highways, bridge approaches, and public works (33 United States Code 701r).

24. Assistance to States and local interests in the development of water supplies for municipal and industrial purposes in connection with Army Corps of Engineers reservoir projects (Water Supply Act of 1958, 43 United States Code 390b).

25. Army Corps of Engineers contracts for remedial works under authority of Section 111 of Act of July 3, 1958 (33 United States Code 633).

TITLE II—INJUNCTIVE RELIEF AGAINST DISCRIMINATION IN PLACES OF PUBLIC ACCOMMODATION

SEC. 201. (a) All persons shall be entitled to the full and equal enjoyment of the goods, services, facilities, privileges, advantages, and accommodations of any place of public accommodation, as defined in this section, without discrimination or segregation on the ground of race, color, religion, or national origin.

Equal access.

(b) Each of the following establishments which serves the public is a place of public accommodation within the meaning of this title if its operations affect commerce, or if discrimination or segregation by it is supported by State action:

Establishments affecting interstate commerce.

(1) any inn, hotel, motel, or other establishment which provides lodging to transient guests, other than an establishment located within a building which contains not more than five rooms for rent or hire and which is actually occupied by the proprietor of such establishment as his residence;

Lodgings.

(2) any restaurant, cafeteria, lunchroom, lunch counter, soda fountain, or other facility principally engaged in selling food for consumption on the premises, including, but not limited to, any such facility located on the premises of any retail establishment; or any gasoline station;

Restaurants, etc.

(3) any motion picture house, theater, concert hall, sports arena, stadium or other place of exhibition or entertainment; and

Theaters, stadiums, etc.

(4) any establishment (A)(i) which is physically located within the premises of any establishment otherwise covered by this subsection, or (ii) within the premises of which is physically located any such covered establishment, and (B) which holds itself out as serving patrons of such covered establishment.

Other covered establishments.

(c) The operations of an establishment affect commerce within the meaning of this title if (1) it is one of the establishments described in paragraph (1) of subsection (b); (2) in the case of an establishment described in paragraph (2) of subsection (b), it serves or offers to serve interstate travelers or a substantial portion of the food which it serves, or gasoline or other products which it sells, has moved in commerce; (3) in the case of an establishment described in paragraph (3) of subsection (b), it customarily presents films, performances, athletic teams, exhibitions, or other sources of entertainment which move in commerce; and (4) in the case of an establishment described in paragraph (4) of subsection (b), it is physically located within the premises of, or there is physically located within its premises, an establishment the operations of which affect commerce within the meaning of this subsection. For purposes of this section, "commerce" means travel, trade, traffic, commerce, transportation, or communication among the several States, or between the District of Columbia and any State, or between any foreign country or any territory or possession and any State or the District of Columbia, or between points in the same State but through any other State or the District of Columbia or a foreign country.

Operations affecting commerce criteria.

"Commerce."

(d) Discrimination or segregation by an establishment is supported by State action within the meaning of this title if such discrimination or segregation (1) is carried on under color of any law, statute, ordinance, or regulation; or (2) is carried on under color of any custom or usage required or enforced by officials of the State or political subdivision thereof; or (3) is required by action of the State or political subdivision thereof.

Support by State action.

(e) The provisions of this title shall not apply to a private club or other establishment not in fact open to the public, except to the extent that the facilities of such establishment are made available

Private establishments.

162

to the customers or patrons of an establishment within the scope of subsection (b).

Entitlement.

SEC. 202. All persons shall be entitled to be free, at any establishment or place, from discrimination or segregation of any kind on the ground of race, color, religion, or national origin, if such discrimination or segregation is or purports to be required by any law, statute, ordinance, regulation, rule, or order of a State or any agency or political subdivision thereof.

Interference.

SEC. 203. No person shall (a) withhold, deny, or attempt to withhold or deny, or deprive or attempt to deprive, any person of any right or privilege secured by section 201 or 202, or (b) intimidate, threaten, or coerce, or attempt to intimidate, threaten, or coerce any person with the purpose of interfering with any right or privilege secured by section 201 or 202, or (c) punish or attempt to punish any person for exercising or attempting to exercise any right or privilege secured by section 201 or 202.

Restraining orders, etc.

SEC. 204. (a) Whenever any person has engaged or there are reasonable grounds to believe that any person is about to engage in any act or practice prohibited by section 203, a civil action for preventive relief, including an application for a permanent or temporary injunction, restraining order, or other order, may be instituted by the person aggrieved and, upon timely application, the court may, in its discretion, permit the Attorney General to intervene in such civil action if he certifies that the case is of general public importance. Upon application by the complainant and in such circumstances as the court may deem just, the court may appoint an attorney for such complainant and may authorize the commencement of the civil action without the payment of fees, costs, or security.

Attorneys' fees.

(b) In any action commenced pursuant to this title, the court, in its discretion, may allow the prevailing party, other than the United States, a reasonable attorney's fee as part of the costs, and the United States shall be liable for costs the same as a private person.

Notification of State.

(c) In the case of an alleged act or practice prohibited by this title which occurs in a State, or political subdivision of a State, which has a State or local law prohibiting such act or practice and establishing or authorizing a State or local authority to grant or seek relief from such practice or to institute criminal proceedings with respect thereto upon receiving notice thereof, no civil action may be brought under subsection (a) before the expiration of thirty days after written notice of such alleged act or practice has been given to the appropriate State or local authority by registered mail or in person, provided that the court may stay proceedings in such civil action pending the termination of State or local enforcement proceedings.

Community Relations Service.

(d) In the case of an alleged act or practice prohibited by this title which occurs in a State, or political subdivision of a State, which has no State or local law prohibiting such act or practice, a civil action may be brought under subsection (a): *Provided*, That the court may refer the matter to the Community Relations Service established by title X of this Act for as long as the court believes there is a reasonable possibility of obtaining voluntary compliance, but for not more than sixty days: *Provided further*, That upon expiration of such sixty-day period, the court may extend such period for an additional period, not to exceed a cumulative total of one hundred and twenty days, if it believes there then exists a reasonable possibility of securing voluntary compliance.

Hearings and investigations.

SEC. 205. The Service is authorized to make a full investigation of any complaint referred to it by the court under section 204(d) and may hold such hearings with respect thereto as may be necessary.

63

The Service shall conduct any hearings with respect to any such complaint in executive session, and shall not release any testimony given therein except by agreement of all parties involved in the complaint with the permission of the court, and the Service shall endeavor to bring about a voluntary settlement between the parties.

Suits by Attorney General.

SEC. 206. (a) Whenever the Attorney General has reasonable cause to believe that any person or group of persons is engaged in a pattern or practice of resistance to the full enjoyment of any of the rights secured by this title, and that the pattern or practice is of such a nature and is intended to deny the full exercise of the rights herein described, the Attorney General may bring a civil action in the appropriate district court of the United States by filing with it a complaint (1) signed by him (or in his absence the Acting Attorney General), (2) setting forth facts pertaining to such pattern or practice, and (3) requesting such preventive relief, including an application for a permanent or temporary injunction, restraining order or other order against the person or persons responsible for such pattern or practice, as he deems necessary to insure the full enjoyment of the rights herein described.

(b) In any such proceeding the Attorney General may file with the clerk of such court a request that a court of three judges be convened to hear and determine the case. Such request by the Attorney General shall be accompanied by a certificate that, in his opinion, the case is of general public importance. A copy of the certificate and request for a three-judge court shall be immediately furnished by such clerk to the chief judge of the circuit (or in his absence, the presiding circuit judge of the circuit) in which the case is pending. Upon receipt of the copy of such request it shall be the duty of the chief judge of the circuit or the presiding circuit judge, as the case may be, to designate immediately three judges in such circuit, of whom at least one shall be a circuit judge and another of whom shall be a district judge of the court in which the proceeding was instituted, to hear and determine such case, and it shall be the duty of the judges so designated to assign the case for hearing at the earliest practicable date, to participate in the hearing and determination thereof, and to cause the case to be in every way expedited. An appeal from the final judgment of such court will lie to the Supreme Court.

Designation of judges.

Appeals.

In the event the Attorney General fails to file such a request in any such proceeding, it shall be the duty of the chief judge of the district (or in his absence, the acting chief judge) in which the case is pending immediately to designate a judge in such district to hear and determine the case. In the event that no judge in the district is available to hear and determine the case, the chief judge of the district, or the acting chief judge, as the case may be, shall certify this fact to the chief judge of the circuit (or in his absence, the acting chief judge) who shall then designate a district or circuit judge of the circuit to hear and determine the case.

It shall be the duty of the judge designated pursuant to this section to assign the case for hearing at the earliest practicable date and to cause the case to be in every way expedited.

District courts, jurisdiction.

SEC. 207. (a) The district courts of the United States shall have jurisdiction of proceedings instituted pursuant to this title and shall exercise the same without regard to whether the aggrieved party shall have exhausted any administrative or other remedies that may be provided by law.

64

Enforcement.

(b) The remedies provided in this title shall be the exclusive means of enforcing the rights based on this title, but nothing in this title shall preclude any individual or any State or local agency from asserting any right based on any other Federal or State law not inconsistent with this title, including any statute or ordinance requiring nondiscrimination in public establishments or accommodations, or from pursuing any remedy, civil or criminal, which may be available for the vindication or enforcement of such right.

TITLE III—DESEGREGATION OF PUBLIC FACILITIES

Suits by Attorney General.

SEC. 301. (a) Whenever the Attorney General receives a complaint in writing signed by an individual to the effect that he is being deprived of or threatened with the loss of his right to the equal protection of the laws, on account of his race, color, religion, or national origin, by being denied equal utilization of any public facility which is owned, operated, or managed by or on behalf of any State or subdivision thereof, other than a public school or public college as defined in section 401 of title IV hereof, and the Attorney General believes the complaint is meritorious and certifies that the signer or signers of such complaint are unable, in his judgment, to initiate and maintain appropriate legal proceedings for relief and that the institution of an action will materially further the orderly progress of desegregation in public facilities, the Attorney General is authorized to institute for or in the name of the United States a civil action in any appropriate district court of the United States against such parties and for such relief as may be appropriate, and such court shall have and shall exercise jurisdiction of proceedings instituted pursuant to this section. The Attorney General may implead as defendants such additional parties as are or become necessary to the grant of effective relief hereunder.

(b) The Attorney General may deem a person or persons unable to initiate and maintain appropriate legal proceedings within the meaning of subsection (a) of this section when such person or persons are unable, either directly or through other interested persons or organizations, to bear the expense of the litigation or to obtain effective legal representation; or whenever he is satisfied that the institution of such litigation would jeopardize the personal safety, employment, or economic standing of such person or persons, their families, or their property.

Costs, fees.

SEC. 302. In any action or proceeding under this title the United States shall be liable for costs, including a reasonable attorney's fee, the same as a private person.

SEC. 303. Nothing in this title shall affect adversely the right of any person to sue for or obtain relief in any court against discrimination in any facility covered by this title.

62 Stat. 749.

SEC. 304. A complaint as used in this title is a writing or document within the meaning of section 1001, title 18, United States Code.

TITLE IV—DESEGREGATION OF PUBLIC EDUCATION

DEFINITIONS

SEC. 401. As used in this title—

"Commissioner."

(a) "Commissioner" means the Commissioner of Education.

"Desegregation."

(b) "Desegregation" means the assignment of students to public schools and within such schools without regard to their race, color, religion, or national origin, but "desegregation" shall not mean the assignment of students to public schools in order to overcome racial imbalance.

65

"Public school."

(c) "Public school" means any elementary or secondary educational institution, and "public college" means any institution of higher education or any technical or vocational school above the secondary school level, provided that such public school or public college is operated by a State, subdivision of a State, or governmental agency within a State, or operated wholly or predominantly from or through the use of governmental funds or property, or funds or property derived from a governmental source.

"School board."

(d) "School board" means any agency or agencies which administer a system of one or more public schools and any other agency which is responsible for the assignment of students to or within such system.

SURVEY AND REPORT OF EDUCATIONAL OPPORTUNITIES

Report to the President and Congress.

SEC. 402. The Commissioner shall conduct a survey and make a report to the President and the Congress, within two years of the enactment of this title, concerning the lack of availability of equal educational opportunities for individuals by reason of race, color, religion, or national origin in public educational institutions at all levels in the United States, its territories and possessions, and the District of Columbia.

TECHNICAL ASSISTANCE

SEC. 403. The Commissioner is authorized, upon the application of any school board, State, municipality, school district, or other governmental unit legally responsible for operating a public school or schools, to render technical assistance to such applicant in the preparation, adoption, and implementation of plans for the desegregation of public schools. Such technical assistance may, among other activities, include making available to such agencies information regarding effective methods of coping with special educational problems occasioned by desegregation, and making available to such agencies personnel of the Office of Education or other persons specially equipped to advise and assist them in coping with such problems.

TRAINING INSTITUTES

SEC. 404. The Commissioner is authorized to arrange, through grants or contracts, with institutions of higher education for the operation of short-term or regular session institutes for special training designed to improve the ability of teachers, supervisors, counselors, and other elementary or secondary school personnel to deal effectively with special educational problems occasioned by desegregation. Individuals who attend such an institute on a full-time basis may be paid stipends for the period of their attendance at such institute in amounts specified by the Commissioner in regulations, including allowances for travel to attend such institute.

Stipends, etc.

GRANTS

SEC. 405. (a) The Commissioner is authorized, upon application of a school board, to make grants to such board to pay, in whole or in part, the cost of—

(1) giving to teachers and other school personnel inservice training in dealing with problems incident to desegregation, and

(2) employing specialists to advise in problems incident to desegregation.

Conditions.

(b) In determining whether to make a grant, and in fixing the amount thereof and the terms and conditions on which it will be made, the Commissioner shall take into consideration the amount available

31-667 O-65—19

66

for grants under this section and the other applications which are pending before him; the financial condition of the applicant and the other resources available to it; the nature, extent, and gravity of its problems incident to desegregation; and such other factors as he finds relevant.

PAYMENTS

SEC. 406. Payments pursuant to a grant or contract under this title may be made (after necessary adjustments on account of previously made overpayments or underpayments) in advance or by way of reimbursement, and in such installments, as the Commissioner may determine.

SUITS BY THE ATTORNEY GENERAL

SEC. 407. (a) Whenever the Attorney General receives a complaint in writing—

(1) signed by a parent or group of parents to the effect that his or their minor children, as members of a class of persons similarly situated, are being deprived by a school board of the equal protection of the laws, or

(2) signed by an individual, or his parent, to the effect that he has been denied admission to or not permitted to continue in attendance at a public college by reason of race, color, religion, or national origin,

and the Attorney General believes the complaint is meritorious and certifies that the signer or signers of such complaint are unable, in his judgment, to initiate and maintain appropriate legal proceedings for relief and that the institution of an action will materially further the orderly achievement of desegregation in public education, the Attorney General is authorized, after giving notice of such complaint to the appropriate school board or college authority and after certifying that he is satisfied that such board or authority has had a reasonable time to adjust the conditions alleged in such complaint, to institute for or in the name of the United States a civil action in any appropriate district court of the United States against such parties and for such relief as may be appropriate, and such court shall have and shall exercise jurisdiction of proceedings instituted pursuant to this section, provided that nothing herein shall empower any official or court of the United States to issue any order seeking to achieve a racial balance in any school by requiring the transportation of pupils or students from one school to another or one school district to another in order to achieve such racial balance, or otherwise enlarge the existing power of the court to insure compliance with constitutional standards. The Attorney General may implead as defendants such additional parties as are or become necessary to the grant of effective relief hereunder.

Persons unable to initiate suits.

(b) The Attorney General may deem a person or persons unable to initiate and maintain appropriate legal proceedings within the meaning of subsection (a) of this section when such person or persons are unable, either directly or through other interested persons or organizations, to bear the expense of the litigation or to obtain effective legal representation; or whenever he is satisfied that the institution of such litigation would jeopardize the personal safety, employment, or economic standing of such person or persons, their families, or their property.

"Parent."
"Complaint."

62 Stat. 749.

(c) The term "parent" as used in this section includes any person standing in loco parentis. A "complaint" as used in this section is a writing or document within the meaning of section 1001, title 18, United States Code.

611

SEC. 408. In any action or proceeding under this title the United States shall be liable for costs the same as a private person.

SEC. 409. Nothing in this title shall affect adversely the right of any person to sue for or obtain relief in any court against discrimination in public education.

SEC. 410. Nothing in this title shall prohibit classification and assignment for reasons other than race, color, religion, or national origin.

TITLE V—COMMISSION ON CIVIL RIGHTS

SEC. 501. Section 102 of the Civil Rights Act of 1957 (42 U.S.C. 1975a; 71 Stat. 634) is amended to read as follows:

"RULES OF PROCEDURE OF THE COMMISSION HEARINGS

Publication in Federal Register.

"SEC. 102. (a) At least thirty days prior to the commencement of any hearing, the Commission shall cause to be published in the Federal Register notice of the date on which such hearing is to commence, the place at which it is to be held and the subject of the hearing. The Chairman, or one designated by him to act as Chairman at a hearing of the Commission, shall announce in an opening statement the subject of the hearing.

"(b) A copy of the Commission's rules shall be made available to any witness before the Commission, and a witness compelled to appear before the Commission or required to produce written or other matter shall be served with a copy of the Commission's rules at the time of service of the subpena.

Right of counsel.

"(c) Any person compelled to appear in person before the Commission shall be accorded the right to be accompanied and advised by counsel, who shall have the right to subject his client to reasonable examination, and to make objections on the record and to argue briefly the basis for such objections. The Commission shall proceed with reasonable dispatch to conclude any hearing in which it is engaged. Due regard shall be had for the convenience and necessity of witnesses.

"(d) The Chairman or Acting Chairman may punish breaches of order and decorum by censure and exclusion from the hearings.

Executive sessions.

"(e) If the Commission determines that evidence or testimony at any hearing may tend to defame, degrade, or incriminate any person, it shall receive such evidence or testimony or summary of such evidence or testimony in executive session. The Commission shall afford any person defamed, degraded, or incriminated by such evidence or testimony an opportunity to appear and be heard in executive session, with a reasonable number of additional witnesses requested by him, before deciding to use such evidence or testimony. In the event the Commission determines to release or use such evidence or testimony in such manner as to reveal publicly the identity of the person defamed, degraded, or incriminated, such evidence or testimony, prior to such public release or use, shall be given at a public session, and the Commission shall afford such person an opportunity to appear as a voluntary witness or to file a sworn statement in his behalf and to submit brief and pertinent sworn statements of others. The Commission shall receive and dispose of requests from such person to subpena additional witnesses.

"(f) Except as provided in sections 102 and 105(f) of this Act, the Chairman shall receive and the Commission shall dispose of requests to subpena additional witnesses.

Testimony, release restrictions.

"(g) No evidence or testimony or summary of evidence or testimony taken in executive session may be released or used in public

68

sessions without the consent of the Commission. Whoever releases or uses in public without the consent of the Commission such evidence or testimony taken in executive session shall be fined not more than $1,000, or imprisoned for not more than one year.

"(h) In the discretion of the Commission, witnesses may submit brief and pertinent sworn statements in writing for inclusion in the record. The Commission shall determine the pertinency of testimony and evidence adduced at its hearings.

Transcript copies.

"(i) Every person who submits data or evidence shall be entitled to retain or, on payment of lawfully prescribed costs, procure a copy or transcript thereof, except that a witness in a hearing held in executive session may for good cause be limited to inspection of the official transcript of his testimony. Transcript copies of public sessions may be obtained by the public upon the payment of the cost thereof. An accurate transcript shall be made of the testimony of all witnesses at all hearings, either public or executive sessions, of the Commission or of any subcommittee thereof.

Witness fees.

"(j) A witness attending any session of the Commission shall receive $6 for each day's attendance and for the time necessarily occupied in going to and returning from the same, and 10 cents per mile for going from and returning to his place of residence. Witnesses who attend at points so far removed from their respective residences as to prohibit return thereto from day to day shall be entitled to an additional allowance of $10 per day for expenses of subsistence, including the time necessarily occupied in going to and returning from the place of attendance. Mileage payments shall be tendered to the witness upon service of a subpena issued on behalf of the Commission or any subcommittee thereof.

Subpena of witnesses.

"(k) The Commission shall not issue any subpena for the attendance and testimony of witnesses or for the production of written or other matter which would require the presence of the party subpenaed at a hearing to be held outside of the State wherein the witness is found or resides or is domiciled or transacts business, or has appointed an agent for receipt of service of process except that, in any event, the Commission may issue subpenas for the attendance and testimony of witnesses and the production of written or other matter at a hearing held within fifty miles of the place where the witness is found or resides or is domiciled or transacts business or has appointed an agent for receipt of service of process.

Organization statement, etc. Publication in Federal Register.

"(l) The Commission shall separately state and currently publish in the Federal Register (1) descriptions of its central and field organization including the established places at which, and methods whereby, the public may secure information or make requests; (2) statements of the general course and method by which its functions are channeled and determined, and (3) rules adopted as authorized by law. No person shall in any manner be subject to or required to resort to rules, organization, or procedure not so published."

SEC. 502. Section 103(a) of the Civil Rights Act of 1957 (42 U.S.C. 1975b(a); 71 Stat. 634) is amended to read as follows:

Payments to members.

"SEC. 103. (a) Each member of the Commission who is not otherwise in the service of the Government of the United States shall receive the sum of $75 per day for each day spent in the work of the Commission, shall be paid actual travel expenses, and per diem in lieu of subsistence expenses when away from his usual place of residence, in accordance with section 5 of the Administrative Expenses Act of 1946, as amended (5 U.S.C. 73b–2; 60 Stat. 808)."

75 Stat. 339, 340.

69.

SEC. 503. Section 103(b) of the Civil Rights Act of 1957 (42 U.S.C. 1975b(b); 71 Stat. 634) is amended to read as follows:

"(b) Each member of the Commission who is otherwise in the service of the Government of the United States shall serve without compensation in addition to that received for such other service, but while engaged in the work of the Commission shall be paid actual travel expenses, and per diem in lieu of subsistence expenses when away from his usual place of residence, in accordance with the provisions of the Travel Expenses Act of 1949, as amended (5 U.S.C. 835-42; 63 Stat. 166)."

75 Stat. 339, 340.

SEC. 504. (a) Section 104(a) of the Civil Rights Act of 1957 (42 U.S.C. 1975c(a); 71 Stat. 635), as amended, is further amended to read as follows:

"DUTIES OF THE COMMISSION

"SEC. 104. (a) The Commission shall—

"(1) investigate allegations in writing under oath or affirmation that certain citizens of the United States are being deprived of their right to vote and have that vote counted by reason of their color, race, religion, or national origin; which writing, under oath or affirmation, shall set forth the facts upon which such belief or beliefs are based;

"(2) study and collect information concerning legal developments constituting a denial of equal protection of the laws under the Constitution because of race, color, religion or national origin or in the administration of justice;

"(3) appraise the laws and policies of the Federal Government with respect to denials of equal protection of the laws under the Constitution because of race, color, religion or national origin or in the administration of justice;

"(4) serve as a national clearinghouse for information in respect to denials of equal protection of the laws because of race, color, religion or national origin, including but not limited to the fields of voting, education, housing, employment, the use of public facilities, and transportation, or in the administration of justice;

"(5) investigate allegations, made in writing and under oath or affirmation, that citizens of the United States are unlawfully being accorded or denied the right to vote, or to have their votes properly counted, in any election of presidential electors, Members of the United States Senate, or of the House of Representatives, as a result of any patterns or practice of fraud or discrimination in the conduct of such election; and

"(6) Nothing in this or any other Act shall be construed as authorizing the Commission, its Advisory Committees, or any person under its supervision or control to inquire into or investigate any membership practices or internal operations of any fraternal organization, any college or university fraternity or sorority, any private club or any religious organization."

(b) Section 104(b) of the Civil Rights Act of 1957 (42 U.S.C. 1975c(b); 71 Stat. 635), as amended, is further amended by striking out the present subsection "(b)" and by substituting therefor:

77 Stat. 271.

Reports to the President and Congress.

"(b) The Commission shall submit interim reports to the President and to the Congress at such times as the Commission, the Congress or the President shall deem desirable, and shall submit to the President and to the Congress a final report of its activities, findings, and recommendations not later than January 31, 1968."

SEC. 505. Section 105(a) of the Civil Rights Act of 1957 (42 U.S.C. 1975d(a); 71 Stat. 636) is amended by striking out in the last sentence thereof "$50 per diem" and inserting in lieu thereof "$75 per diem."

70

Powers.

SEC. 506. Section 105(f) and section 105(g) of the Civil Rights Act of 1957 (42 U.S.C. 1975d (f) and (g); 71 Stat. 636) are amended to read as follows:

"(f) The Commission, or on the authorization of the Commission any subcommittee of two or more members, at least one of whom shall be of each major political party, may, for the purpose of carrying out the provisions of this Act, hold such hearings and act at such times and places as the Commission or such authorized subcommittee may deem advisable. Subpenas for the attendance and testimony of witnesses or the production of written or other matter may be issued in accordance with the rules of the Commission as contained in section 102 (j) and (k) of this Act, over the signature of the Chairman of the Commission or of such subcommittee, and may be served by any person designated by such Chairman. The holding of hearings by the Commission, or the appointment of a subcommittee to hold hearings pursuant to this subparagraph, must be approved by a majority of the Commission, or by a majority of the members present at a meeting at which at least a quorum of four members is present.

Ante, p. 250.

"(g) In case of contumacy or refusal to obey a subpena, any district court of the United States or the United States court of any territory or possession, or the District Court of the United States for the District of Columbia, within the jurisdiction of which the inquiry is carried on or within the jurisdiction of which said person guilty of contumacy or refusal to obey is found or resides or is domiciled or transacts business, or has appointed an agent for receipt of service of process, upon application by the Attorney General of the United States shall have jurisdiction to issue to such person an order requiring such person to appear before the Commission or a subcommittee thereof, there to produce pertinent, relevant and nonprivileged evidence if so ordered, or there to give testimony touching the matter under investigation; and any failure to obey such order of the court may be punished by said court as a contempt thereof."

SEC. 507. Section 105 of the Civil Rights Act of 1957 (42 U.S.C. 1975d; 71 Stat. 636), as amended by section 401 of the Civil Rights Act of 1960 (42 U.S.C. 1975d(h); 74 Stat. 89), is further amended by adding a new subsection at the end to read as follows:

"(i) The Commission shall have the power to make such rules and regulations as are necessary to carry out the purposes of this Act."

TITLE VI—NONDISCRIMINATION IN FEDERALLY ASSISTED PROGRAMS

SEC. 601. No person in the United States shall, on the ground of race, color, or national origin, be excluded from participation in, be denied the benefits of, or be subjected to discrimination under any program or activity receiving Federal financial assistance.

Rules governing grants, loans, and contracts.

SEC. 602. Each Federal department and agency which is empowered to extend Federal financial assistance to any program or activity, by way of grant, loan, or contract other than a contract of insurance or guaranty, is authorized and directed to effectuate the provisions of section 601 with respect to such program or activity by issuing rules, regulations, or orders of general applicability which shall be consistent with achievement of the objectives of the statute authorizing the financial assistance in connection with which the action is taken. No such rule, regulation, or order shall become effective unless and until approved by the President. Compliance with any requirement adopted pursuant to this section may be effected (1) by the termination of or refusal to grant or to continue assistance under such program or activity to any recipient as to whom there has been an express find-

Approval by President.

71

ing on the record, after opportunity for hearing, of a failure to comply with such requirement, but such termination or refusal shall be limited to the particular political entity, or part thereof, or other recipient as to whom such a finding has been made and, shall be limited in its effect to the particular program, or part thereof, in which such noncompliance has been so found, or (2) by any other means authorized by law: *Provided, however*, That no such action shall be taken until the department or agency concerned has advised the appropriate person or persons of the failure to comply with the requirement and has determined that compliance cannot be secured by voluntary means. In the case of any action terminating, or refusing to grant or continue, assistance because of failure to comply with a requirement imposed pursuant to this section, the head of the Federal department or agency shall file with the committees of the House and Senate having legislative jurisdiction over the program or activity involved a full written report of the circumstances and the grounds for such action. No such action shall become effective until thirty days have elapsed after the filing of such report.

Termination.

SEC. 603. Any department or agency action taken pursuant to section 602 shall be subject to such judicial review as may otherwise be provided by law for similar action taken by such department or agency on other grounds. In the case of action, not otherwise subject to judicial review, terminating or refusing to grant or to continue financial assistance upon a finding of failure to comply with any requirement imposed pursuant to section 602, any person aggrieved (including any State or political subdivision thereof and any agency of either) may obtain judicial review of such action in accordance with section 10 of the Administrative Procedure Act, and such action shall not be deemed committed to unreviewable agency discretion within the meaning of that section.

Judicial review.

60 Stat. 243.
5 USC 1009.

SEC. 604. Nothing contained in this title shall be construed to authorize action under this title by any department or agency with respect to any employment practice of any employer, employment agency, or labor organization except where a primary objective of the Federal financial assistance is to provide employment.

SEC. 605. Nothing in this title shall add to or detract from any existing authority with respect to any program or activity under which Federal financial assistance is extended by way of a contract of insurance or guaranty.

TITLE VII—EQUAL EMPLOYMENT OPPORTUNITY

DEFINITIONS

SEC. 701. For the purposes of this title—

(a) The term "person" includes one or more individuals, labor unions, partnerships, associations, corporations, legal representatives, mutual companies, joint-stock companies, trusts, unincorporated organizations, trustees, trustees in bankruptcy, or receivers.

"Person."

(b) The term "employer" means a person engaged in an industry affecting commerce who has twenty-five or more employees for each working day in each of twenty or more calendar weeks in the current or preceding calendar year, and any agent of such a person, but such term does not include (1) the United States, a corporation wholly owned by the Government of the United States, an Indian tribe, or a State or political subdivision thereof, (2) a bona fide private membership club (other than a labor organization) which is exempt from taxation under section 501(c) of the Internal Revenue Code of 1954: *Provided*, That during the first year after the effective date prescribed in subsection (a) of section 716, persons having fewer than one hun-

"Employer."

68A Stat. 163;
74 Stat. 534.
26 USC 501.

72

dred employees (and their agents) shall not be considered employers, and, during the second year after such date, persons having fewer than seventy-five employees (and their agents) shall not be considered employers, and, during the third year after such date, persons having fewer than fifty employees (and their agents) shall not be considered employers: *Provided further*, That it shall be the policy of the United States to insure equal employment opportunities for Federal employees without discrimination because of race, color, religion, sex or national origin and the President shall utilize his existing authority to effectuate this policy.

"Employment agency."

(c) The term "employment agency" means any person regularly undertaking with or without compensation to procure employees for an employer or to procure for employees opportunities to work for an employer and includes an agent of such a person; but shall not include an agency of the United States, or an agency of a State or political subdivision of a State, except that such term shall include the United States Employment Service and the system of State and local employment services receiving Federal assistance.

"Labor organization."

(d) The term "labor organization" means a labor organization engaged in an industry affecting commerce, and any agent of such an organization, and includes any organization of any kind, any agency, or employee representation committee, group, association, or plan so engaged in which employees participate and which exists for the purpose, in whole or in part, of dealing with employers concerning grievances, labor disputes, wages, rates of pay, hours, or other terms or conditions of employment, and any conference, general committee, joint or system board, or joint council so engaged which is subordinate to a national or international labor organization.

(e) A labor organization shall be deemed to be engaged in an industry affecting commerce if (1) it maintains or operates a hiring hall or hiring office which procures employees for an employer or procures for employees opportunities to work for an employer, or (2) the number of its members (or, where it is a labor organization composed of other labor organizations or their representatives, if the aggregate number of the members of such other labor organization) is (A) one hundred or more during the first year after the effective date prescribed in subsection (a) of section 716, (B) seventy-five or more during the second year after such date or fifty or more during the third year, or (C) twenty-five or more thereafter, and such labor organization—

61 Stat. 136.
29 USC 167.
44 Stat. 577;
49 Stat. 1189.
45 USC 151.

(1) is the certified representative of employees under the provisions of the National Labor Relations Act, as amended, or the Railway Labor Act, as amended;

(2) although not certified, is a national or international labor organization or a local labor organization recognized or acting as the representative of employees of an employer or employers engaged in an industry affecting commerce; or

(3) has chartered a local labor organization or subsidiary body which is representing or actively seeking to represent employees of employers within the meaning of paragraph (1) or (2); or

(4) has been chartered by a labor organization representing or actively seeking to represent employees within the meaning of paragraph (1) or (2) as the local or subordinate body through which such employees may enjoy membership or become affiliated with such labor organization; or

(5) is a conference, general committee, joint or system board, or joint council subordinate to a national or international labor organization, which includes a labor organization engaged in an

0073

industry affecting commerce within the meaning of any of the preceding paragraphs of this subsection.

(f) The term "employee" means an individual employed by an employer.

"Employee."

(g) The term "commerce" means trade, traffic, commerce, transportation, transmission, or communication among the several States; or between a State and any place outside thereof; or within the District of Columbia, or a possession of the United States; or between points in the same State but through a point outside thereof.

"Commerce."

(h) The term "industry affecting commerce" means any activity, business, or industry in commerce or in which a labor dispute would hinder or obstruct commerce or the free flow of commerce and includes any activity or industry "affecting commerce" within the meaning of the Labor-Management Reporting and Disclosure Act of 1959.

"Industry affecting commerce."

73 Stat. 519. 29 USC 401 note.

(i) The term "State" includes a State of the United States, the District of Columbia, Puerto Rico, the Virgin Islands, American Samoa, Guam, Wake Island, the Canal Zone, and Outer Continental Shelf lands defined in the Outer Continental Shelf Lands Act.

"State."

67 Stat. 462. 43 USC 1331 note.

EXEMPTION

SEC. 702. This title shall not apply to an employer with respect to the employment of aliens outside any State, or to a religious corporation, association, or society with respect to the employment of individuals of a particular religion to perform work connected with the carrying on by such corporation, association, or society of its religious activities or to an educational institution with respect to the employment of individuals to perform work connected with the educational activities of such institution.

Religious organizations, etc.

DISCRIMINATION BECAUSE OF RACE, COLOR, RELIGION, SEX, OR NATIONAL ORIGIN

SEC. 703. (a) It shall be an unlawful employment practice for an employer—

Unlawful practices.

Employers.

(1) to fail or refuse to hire or to discharge any individual, or otherwise to discriminate against any individual with respect to his compensation, terms, conditions, or privileges of employment, because of such individual's race, color, religion, sex, or national origin; or

(2) to limit, segregate, or classify his employees in any way which would deprive or tend to deprive any individual of employment opportunities or otherwise adversely affect his status as an employee, because of such individual's race, color, religion, sex, or national origin.

(b) It shall be an unlawful employment practice for an employment agency to fail or refuse to refer for employment, or otherwise to discriminate against, any individual because of his race, color, religion, sex, or national origin, or to classify or refer for employment any individual on the basis of his race, color, religion, sex, or national origin.

Employment agency.

(c) It shall be an unlawful employment practice for a labor organization—

Labor organization.

(1) to exclude or to expel from its membership, or otherwise to discriminate against, any individual because of his race, color, religion, sex, or national origin;

(2) to limit, segregate, or classify its membership, or to classify or fail or refuse to refer for employment any individual, in any

74

way which would deprive or tend to deprive any individual of employment opportunities, or would limit such employment opportunities or otherwise adversely affect his status as an employee or as an applicant for employment, because of such individual's race, color, religion, sex, or national origin; or

(3) to cause or attempt to cause an employer to discriminate against an individual in violation of this section.

Training programs.

(d) It shall be an unlawful employment practice for any employer, labor organization, or joint labor-management committee controlling apprenticeship or other training or retraining, including on-the-job training programs to discriminate against any individual because of his race, color, religion, sex, or national origin in admission to, or employment in, any program established to provide apprenticeship or other training.

Exceptions.

(e) Notwithstanding any other provision of this title, (1) it shall not be an unlawful employment practice for an employer to hire and employ employees, for an employment agency to classify, or refer for employment any individual, for a labor organization to classify its membership or to classify or refer for employment any individual, or for an employer, labor organization, or joint labor-management committee controlling apprenticeship or other training or retraining programs to admit or employ any individual in any such program, on the basis of his religion, sex, or national origin in those certain instances where religion, sex, or national origin is a bona fide occupational qualification reasonably necessary to the normal operation of that particular business or enterprise, and (2) it shall not be an unlawful employment practice for a school, college, university, or other educational institution or institution of learning to hire and employ employees of a particular religion if such school, college, university, or other educational institution or institution of learning is, in whole or in substantial part, owned, supported, controlled, or managed by a particular religion or by a particular religious corporation, association, or society, or if the curriculum of such school, college, university, or other educational institution or institution of learning is directed toward the propagation of a particular religion.

(f) As used in this title, the phrase "unlawful employment practice" shall not be deemed to include any action or measure taken by an employer, labor organization, joint labor-management committee, or employment agency with respect to an individual who is a member of the Communist Party of the United States or of any other organization required to register as a Communist-action or Communist-front organization by final order of the Subversive Activities Control Board pursuant to the Subversive Activities Control Act of 1950.

64 Stat. 987. 50 USC 781 note.

(g) Notwithstanding any other provision of this title, it shall not be an unlawful employment practice for an employer to fail or refuse to hire and employ any individual for any position, for an employer to discharge any individual from any position, or for an employment agency to fail or refuse to refer any individual for employment in any position, or for a labor organization to fail or refuse to refer any individual for employment in any position, if—

(1) the occupancy of such position, or access to the premises in or upon which any part of the duties of such position is performed or is to be performed, is subject to any requirement imposed in the interest of the national security of the United States under any security program in effect pursuant to or administered under any statute of the United States or any Executive order of the President; and

(2) such individual has not fulfilled or has ceased to fulfill that requirement.

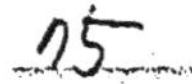

(h) Notwithstanding any other provision of this title, it shall not be an unlawful employment practice for an employer to apply different standards of compensation, or different terms, conditions, or privileges of employment pursuant to a bona fide seniority or merit system, or a system which measures earnings by quantity or quality of production or to employees who work in different locations, provided that such differences are not the result of an intention to discriminate because of race, color, religion, sex, or national origin, nor shall it be an unlawful employment practice for an employer to give and to act upon the results of any professionally developed ability test provided that such test, its administration or action upon the results is not designed, intended or used to discriminate because of race, color, religion, sex or national origin. It shall not be an unlawful employment practice under this title for any employer to differentiate upon the basis of sex in determining the amount of the wages or compensation paid or to be paid to employees of such employer if such differentiation is authorized by the provisions of section 6(d) of the Fair Labor Standards Act of 1938, as amended (29 U.S.C. 206(d)).

77 Stat. 56.
29 USC 206.
Indians.

(i) Nothing contained in this title shall apply to any business or enterprise on or near an Indian reservation with respect to any publicly announced employment practice of such business or enterprise under which a preferential treatment is given to any individual because he is an Indian living on or near a reservation.

Preferential treatment.

(j) Nothing contained in this title shall be interpreted to require any employer, employment agency, labor organization, or joint labor-management committee subject to this title to grant preferential treatment to any individual or to any group because of the race, color, religion, sex, or national origin of such individual or group on account of an imbalance which may exist with respect to the total number or percentage of persons of any race, color, religion, sex, or national origin employed by any employer, referred or classified for employment by any employment agency or labor organization, admitted to membership or classified by any labor organization, or admitted to, or employed in, any apprenticeship or other training program, in comparison with the total number or percentage of persons of such race, color, religion, sex, or national origin in any community, State, section, or other area, or in the available work force in any community, State, section, or other area.

OTHER UNLAWFUL EMPLOYMENT PRACTICES

SEC. 704. (a) It shall be an unlawful employment practice for an employer to discriminate against any of his employees or applicants for employment, for an employment agency to discriminate against any individual, or for a labor organization to discriminate against any member thereof or applicant for membership, because he has opposed any practice made an unlawful employment practice by this title, or because he has made a charge, testified, assisted, or participated in any manner in an investigation, proceeding, or hearing under this title.

(b) It shall be an unlawful employment practice for an employer, labor organization, or employment agency to print or publish or cause to be printed or published any notice or advertisement relating to employment by such an employer or membership in or any classification or referral for employment by such a labor organization, or relating to any classification or referral for employment by such an employment agency, indicating any preference, limitation, specification, or discrimination, based on race, color, religion, sex, or national origin, except that such a notice or advertisement may indicate a preference, limitation, specification, or discrimination based on reli-

76

gion, sex, or national origin when religion, sex, or national origin is a bona fide occupational qualification for employment.

EQUAL EMPLOYMENT OPPORTUNITY COMMISSION

Establishment.

SEC. 705. (a) There is hereby created a Commission to be known as the Equal Employment Opportunity Commission, which shall be composed of five members, not more than three of whom shall be members of the same political party, who shall be appointed by the President by and with the advice and consent of the Senate. One of the original members shall be appointed for a term of one year, one for a term of two years, one for a term of three years, one for a term of four years, and one for a term of five years, beginning from the date of enactment of this title, but their successors shall be appointed for terms of five years each, except that any individual chosen to fill a vacancy shall be appointed only for the unexpired term of the member whom he shall succeed. The President shall designate one member to serve as Chairman of the Commission, and one member to serve as Vice Chairman. The Chairman shall be responsible on behalf of the Commission for the administrative operations of the Commission, and shall appoint, in accordance with the civil service laws, such officers, agents, attorneys, and employees as it deems necessary to assist it in the performance of its functions and to fix their compensation in accordance with the Classification Act of 1949, as amended. The Vice Chairman shall act as Chairman in the absence or disability of the Chairman or in the event of a vacancy in that office.

Term of office.

Post, p. 400. 5 U.S.C. 1071 note.

(b) A vacancy in the Commission shall not impair the right of the remaining members to exercise all the powers of the Commission and three members thereof shall constitute a quorum.

(c) The Commission shall have an official seal which shall be judicially noticed.

Reports to the President and Congress.

(d) The Commission shall at the close of each fiscal year report to the Congress and to the President concerning the action it has taken; the names, salaries, and duties of all individuals in its employ and the moneys it has disbursed; and shall make such further reports on the cause of and means of eliminating discrimination and such recommendations for further legislation as may appear desirable.

70 Stat. 736. 5 USC 2201 note.

(e) The Federal Executive Pay Act of 1956, as amended (5 U.S.C. 2201–2209), is further amended—

(1) by adding to section 105 thereof (5 U.S.C. 2204) the following clause:

"(32) Chairman, Equal Employment Opportunity Commission"; and

70 Stat. 737. 5 USC 2205.

(2) by adding to clause (45) of section 106(a) thereof (5 U.S.C. 2205(a)) the following: "Equal Employment Opportunity Commission (4)."

(f) The principal office of the Commission shall be in or near the District of Columbia, but it may meet or exercise any or all its powers at any other place. The Commission may establish such regional or State offices as it deems necessary to accomplish the purpose of this title.

Powers.

(g) The Commission shall have power—

(1) to cooperate with and, with their consent, utilize regional, State, local, and other agencies, both public and private, and individuals;

(2) to pay to witnesses whose depositions are taken or who are summoned before the Commission or any of its agents the same witness and mileage fees as are paid to witnesses in the courts of the United States;

(3) to furnish to persons subject to this title such technical assistance as they may request to further their compliance with this title or an order issued thereunder;

(4) upon the request of (i) any employer, whose employees or some of them, or (ii) any labor organization, whose members or some of them, refuse or threaten to refuse to cooperate in effectuating the provisions of this title, to assist in such effectuation by conciliation or such other remedial action as is provided by this title;

(5) to make such technical studies as are appropriate to effectuate the purposes and policies of this title and to make the results of such studies available to the public;

(6) to refer matters to the Attorney General with recommendations for intervention in a civil action brought by an aggrieved party under section 706, or for the institution of a civil action by the Attorney General under section 707, and to advise, consult, and assist the Attorney General on such matters.

(h) Attorneys appointed under this section may, at the direction of the Commission, appear for and represent the Commission in any case in court.

(i) The Commission shall, in any of its educational or promotional activities, cooperate with other departments and agencies in the performance of such educational and promotional activities.

(j) All officers, agents, attorneys, and employees of the Commission shall be subject to the provisions of section 9 of the Act of August 2, 1939, as amended (the Hatch Act), notwithstanding any exemption contained in such section.

53 Stat. 1148; 64 Stat. 475. 5 USC 118i.

PREVENTION OF UNLAWFUL EMPLOYMENT PRACTICES

SEC. 706. (a) Whenever it is charged in writing under oath by a person claiming to be aggrieved, or a written charge has been filed by a member of the Commission where he has reasonable cause to believe a violation of this title has occurred (and such charge sets forth the facts upon which it is based) that an employer, employment agency, or labor organization has engaged in an unlawful employment practice, the Commission shall furnish such employer, employment agency, or labor organization (hereinafter referred to as the "respondent") with a copy of such charge and shall make an investigation of such charge, provided that such charge shall not be made public by the Commission. If the Commission shall determine, after such investigation, that there is reasonable cause to believe that the charge is true, the Commission shall endeavor to eliminate any such alleged unlawful employment practice by informal methods of conference, conciliation, and persuasion. Nothing said or done during and as a part of such endeavors may be made public by the Commission without the written consent of the parties, or used as evidence in a subsequent proceeding. Any officer or employee of the Commission, who shall make public in any manner whatever any information in violation of this subsection shall be deemed guilty of a misdemeanor and upon conviction thereof shall be fined not more than $1,000 or imprisoned not more than one year.

Legal proceedings.

(b) In the case of an alleged unlawful employment practice occurring in a State, or political subdivision of a State, which has a State or local law prohibiting the unlawful employment practice alleged and establishing or authorizing a State or local authority to grant or seek relief from such practice or to institute criminal proceedings with respect thereto upon receiving notice thereof, no charge may be filed under subsection (a) by the person aggrieved before the expira-

tion of sixty days after proceedings have been commenced under the State or local law, unless such proceedings have been earlier terminated, provided that such sixty-day period shall be extended to one hundred and twenty days during the first year after the effective date of such State or local law. If any requirement for the commencement of such proceedings is imposed by a State or local authority other than a requirement of the filing of a written and signed statement of the facts upon which the proceeding is based, the proceeding shall be deemed to have been commenced for the purposes of this subsection at the time such statement is sent by registered mail to the appropriate State or local authority.

Time requirements.

(c) In the case of any charge filed by a member of the Commission alleging an unlawful employment practice occurring in a State or political subdivision of a State, which has a State or local law prohibiting the practice alleged and establishing or authorizing a State or local authority to grant or seek relief from such practice or to institute criminal proceedings with respect thereto upon receiving notice thereof, the Commission shall, before taking any action with respect to such charge, notify the appropriate State or local officials and, upon request, afford them a reasonable time, but not less than sixty days (provided that such sixty-day period shall be extended to one hundred and twenty days during the first year after the effective day of such State or local law), unless a shorter period is requested, to act under such State or local law to remedy the practice alleged.

(d) A charge under subsection (a) shall be filed within ninety days after the alleged unlawful employment practice occurred, except that in the case of an unlawful employment practice with respect to which the person aggrieved has followed the procedure set out in subsection (b), such charge shall be filed by the person aggrieved within two hundred and ten days after the alleged unlawful employment practice occurred, or within thirty days after receiving notice that the State or local agency has terminated the proceedings under the State or local law, whichever is earlier, and a copy of such charge shall be filed by the Commission with the State or local agency.

(e) If within thirty days after a charge is filed with the Commission or within thirty days after expiration of any period of reference under subsection (c) (except that in either case such period may be extended to not more than sixty days upon a determination by the Commission that further efforts to secure voluntary compliance are warranted), the Commission has been unable to obtain voluntary compliance with this title, the Commission shall so notify the person aggrieved and a civil action may, within thirty days thereafter, be brought against the respondent named in the charge (1) by the person claiming to be aggrieved, or (2) if such charge was filed by a member of the Commission, by any person whom the charge alleges was aggrieved by the alleged unlawful employment practice. Upon application by the complainant and in such circumstances as the court may deem just, the court may appoint an attorney for such complainant and may authorize the commencement of the action without the payment of fees, costs, or security. Upon timely application, the court may, in its discretion, permit the Attorney General to intervene in such civil action if he certifies that the case is of general public importance. Upon request, the court may, in its discretion, stay further proceedings for not more than sixty days pending the termination of State or local proceedings described in subsection (b) or the efforts of the Commission to obtain voluntary compliance.

Courts. Jurisdiction.

(f) Each United States district court and each United States court of a place subject to the jurisdiction of the United States shall

79

have jurisdiction of actions brought under this title. Such an action may be brought in any judicial district in the State in which the unlawful employment practice is alleged to have been committed, in the judicial district in which the employment records relevant to such practice are maintained and administered, or in the judicial district in which the plaintiff would have worked but for the alleged unlawful employment practice, but if the respondent is not found within any such district, such an action may be brought within the judicial district in which the respondent has his principal office. For purposes of sections 1404 and 1406 of title 28 of the United States Code, the judicial district in which the respondent has his principal office shall in all cases be considered a district in which the action might have been brought.

62 Stat. 937. 74 Stat. 912; 76A Stat. 699.

(g) If the court finds that the respondent has intentionally engaged in or is intentionally engaging in an unlawful employment practice charged in the complaint, the court may enjoin the respondent from engaging in such unlawful employment practice, and order such affirmative action as may be appropriate, which may include reinstatement or hiring of employees, with or without back pay (payable by the employer, employment agency, or labor organization, as the case may be, responsible for the unlawful employment practice). Interim earnings or amounts earnable with reasonable diligence by the person or persons discriminated against shall operate to reduce the back pay otherwise allowable. No order of the court shall require the admission or reinstatement of an individual as a member of a union or the hiring, reinstatement, or promotion of an individual as an employee, or the payment to him of any back pay, if such individual was refused admission, suspended, or expelled or was refused employment or advancement or was suspended or discharged for any reason other than discrimination on account of race, color, religion, sex or national origin or in violation of section 704(a).

(h) The provisions of the Act entitled "An Act to amend the Judicial Code and to define and limit the jurisdiction of courts sitting in equity, and for other purposes," approved March 23, 1932 (29 U.S.C. 101–115), shall not apply with respect to civil actions brought under this section.

47 Stat. 70.

(i) In any case in which an employer, employment agency, or labor organization fails to comply with an order of a court issued in a civil action brought under subsection (e), the Commission may commence proceedings to compel compliance with such order.

(j) Any civil action brought under subsection (e) and any proceedings brought under subsection (i) shall be subject to appeal as provided in sections 1291 and 1292, title 28, United States Code.

62 Stat. 929. 65 Stat. 726; 72 Stat. 348, 1770.

Costs, fees.

(k) In any action or proceeding under this title the court, in its discretion, may allow the prevailing party, other than the Commission or the United States, a reasonable attorney's fee as part of the costs, and the Commission and the United States shall be liable for costs the same as a private person.

Suits by Attorney General.

SEC. 707. (a) Whenever the Attorney General has reasonable cause to believe that any person or group of persons is engaged in a pattern or practice of resistance to the full enjoyment of any of the rights secured by this title, and that the pattern or practice is of such a nature and is intended to deny the full exercise of the rights herein described, the Attorney General may bring a civil action in the appropriate district court of the United States by filing with it a complaint (1) signed by him (or in his absence the Acting Attorney General), (2) setting forth facts pertaining to such pattern or practice, and (3) requesting such relief, including an application for a permanent or temporary injunction, restraining order or other order against the person or persons responsible for such pattern or practice, as he deems necessary to insure the full enjoyment of the rights herein described.

(b) The district courts of the United States shall have and shall exercise jurisdiction of proceedings instituted pursuant to this section, and in any such proceeding the Attorney General may file with the clerk of such court a request that a court of three judges be convened to hear and determine the case. Such request by the Attorney General shall be accompanied by a certificate that, in his opinion, the case is of general public importance. A copy of the certificate and request for a three-judge court shall be immediately furnished by such clerk to the chief judge of the circuit (or in his absence, the presiding circuit judge of the circuit) in which the case is pending. Upon receipt of such request it shall be the duty of the chief judge of the circuit or the presiding circuit judge, as the case may be, to designate immediately three judges in such circuit, of whom at least one shall be a circuit judge and another of whom shall be a district judge of the court in which the proceeding was instituted, to hear and determine such case, and it shall be the duty of the judges so designated to assign the case for hearing at the earliest practicable date, to participate in the hearing and determination thereof, and to cause the case to be in every way expedited. An appeal from the final judgment of such court will lie to the Supreme Court.

In the event the Attorney General fails to file such a request in any such proceeding, it shall be the duty of the chief judge of the district (or in his absence, the acting chief judge) in which the case is pending immediately to designate a judge in such district to hear and determine the case. In the event that no judge in the district is available to hear and determine the case, the chief judge of the district, or the acting chief judge, as the case may be, shall certify this fact to the chief judge of the circuit (or in his absence, the acting chief judge) who shall then designate a district or circuit judge of the circuit to hear and determine the case.

It shall be the duty of the judge designated pursuant to this section to assign the case for hearing at the earliest practicable date and to cause the case to be in every way expedited.

EFFECT ON STATE LAWS

SEC. 708. Nothing in this title shall be deemed to exempt or relieve any person from any liability, duty, penalty, or punishment provided by any present or future law of any State or political subdivision of a State, other than any such law which purports to require or permit the doing of any act which would be an unlawful employment practice under this title.

INVESTIGATIONS, INSPECTIONS, RECORDS, STATE AGENCIES

SEC. 709. (a) In connection with any investigation of a charge filed under section 706, the Commission or its designated representative shall at all reasonable times have access to, for the purposes of examination, and the right to copy any evidence of any person being investigated or proceeded against that relates to unlawful employment practices covered by this title and is relevant to the charge under investigation.

Agreements, State and local agencies.

(b) The Commission may cooperate with State and local agencies charged with the administration of State fair employment practices laws and, with the consent of such agencies, may for the purpose of carrying out its functions and duties under this title and within the limitation of funds appropriated specifically for such purpose, utilize the services of such agencies and their employees and, notwithstand-

81.

ing any other provision of law, may reimburse such agencies and their employees for services rendered to assist the Commission in carrying out this title. In furtherance of such cooperative efforts, the Commission may enter into written agreements with such State or local agencies and such agreements may include provisions under which the Commission shall refrain from processing a charge in any cases or class of cases specified in such agreements and under which no person may bring a civil action under section 706 in any cases or class of cases so specified, or under which the Commission shall relieve any person or class of persons in such State or locality from requirements imposed under this section. The Commission shall rescind any such agreement whenever it determines that the agreement no longer serves the interest of effective enforcement of this title.

Records.

(c) Except as provided in subsection (d), every employer, employment agency, and labor organization subject to this title shall (1) make and keep such records relevant to the determinations of whether unlawful employment practices have been or are being committed, (2) preserve such records for such periods, and (3) make such reports therefrom, as the Commission shall prescribe by regulation or order, after public hearing, as reasonable, necessary, or appropriate for the enforcement of this title or the regulations or orders thereunder. The Commission shall, by regulation, require each employer, labor organization, and joint labor-management committee subject to this title which controls an apprenticeship or other training program to maintain such records as are reasonably necessary to carry out the purpose of this title, including, but not limited to, a list of applicants who wish to participate in such program, including the chronological order in which such applications were received, and shall furnish to the Commission, upon request, a detailed description of the manner in which persons are selected to participate in the apprenticeship or other training program. Any employer, employment agency, labor organization, or joint labor-management committee which believes that the application to it of any regulation or order issued under this section would result in undue hardship may (1) apply to the Commission for an exemption from the application of such regulation or order, or (2) bring a civil action in the United States district court for the district where such records are kept. If the Commission or the court, as the case may be, finds that the application of the regulation or order to the employer, employment agency, or labor organization in question would impose an undue hardship, the Commission or the court, as the case may be, may grant appropriate relief.

Exceptions.

(d) The provisions of subsection (c) shall not apply to any employer, employment agency, labor organization, or joint labor-management committee with respect to matters occurring in any State or political subdivision thereof which has a fair employment practice law during any period in which such employer, employment agency, labor organization, or joint labor-management committee is subject to such law, except that the Commission may require such notations on records which such employer, employment agency, labor organization, or joint labor-management committee keeps or is required to keep as are necessary because of differences in coverage or methods of enforcement between the State or local law and the provisions of this title. Where an employer is required by Executive Order 10925, issued March 6, 1961, or by any other Executive order prescribing fair employment practices for Government contractors and subcontractors, or by rules or regulations issued thereunder, to file reports relating to his employment practices with any Federal agency or committee, and he is substantially in compliance with such requirements, the Commission shall not require him to file additional reports pursuant to subsection (c) of this section.

3 CFR, 1961 Supp., p. 86.
5 USC 631 note.

31-567 O-65—20

82

Prohibited disclosures.

(e) It shall be unlawful for any officer or employee of the Commission to make public in any manner whatever any information obtained by the Commission pursuant to its authority under this section prior to the institution of any proceeding under this title involving such information. Any officer or employee of the Commission who shall make public in any manner whatever any information in violation of this subsection shall be guilty of a misdemeanor and upon conviction thereof, shall be fined not more than $1,000, or imprisoned not more than one year.

INVESTIGATORY POWERS

SEC. 710. (a) For the purposes of any investigation of a charge filed under the authority contained in section 706, the Commission shall have authority to examine witnesses under oath and to require the production of documentary evidence relevant or material to the charge under investigation.

(b) If the respondent named in a charge filed under section 706 fails or refuses to comply with a demand of the Commission for permission to examine or to copy evidence in conformity with the provisions of section 709(a), or if any person required to comply with the provisions of section 709 (c) or (d) fails or refuses to do so, or if any person fails or refuses to comply with a demand by the Commission to give testimony under oath, the United States district court for the district in which such person is found, resides, or transacts business, shall, upon application of the Commission, have jurisdiction to issue to such person an order requiring him to comply with the provisions of section 709 (c) or (d) or to comply with the demand of the Commission, but the attendance of a witness may not be required outside the State where he is found, resides, or transacts business and the production of evidence may not be required outside the State where such evidence is kept.

Petitions.

(c) Within twenty days after the service upon any person charged under section 706 of a demand by the Commission for the production of documentary evidence or for permission to examine or to copy evidence in conformity with the provisions of section 709(a), such person may file in the district court of the United States for the judicial district in which he resides, is found, or transacts business, and serve upon the Commission a petition for an order of such court modifying or setting aside such demand. The time allowed for compliance with the demand in whole or in part as deemed proper and ordered by the court shall not run during the pendency of such petition in the court. Such petition shall specify each ground upon which the petitioner relies in seeking such relief, and may be based upon any failure of such demand to comply with the provisions of this title or with the limitations generally applicable to compulsory process or upon any constitutional or other legal right or privilege of such person. No objection which is not raised by such a petition may be urged in the defense to a proceeding initiated by the Commission under subsection (b) for enforcement of such a demand unless such proceeding is commenced by the Commission prior to the expiration of the twenty-day period, or unless the court determines that the defendant could not reasonably have been aware of the availability of such ground of objection.

(d) In any proceeding brought by the Commission under subsection (b), except as provided in subsection (c) of this section, the defendant may petition the court for an order modifying or setting aside the demand of the Commission.

83

NOTICES TO BE POSTED

SEC. 711. (a) Every employer, employment agency, and labor organization, as the case may be, shall post and keep posted in conspicuous places upon its premises where notices to employees, applicants for employment, and members are customarily posted a notice to be prepared or approved by the Commission setting forth excerpts from or, summaries of, the pertinent provisions of this title and information pertinent to the filing of a complaint.

(b) A willful violation of this section shall be punishable by a fine of not more than $100 for each separate offense.

VETERANS' PREFERENCE

SEC. 712. Nothing contained in this title shall be construed to repeal or modify any Federal, State, territorial, or local law creating special rights or preference for veterans.

RULES AND REGULATIONS

SEC. 713. (a) The Commission shall have authority from time to time to issue, amend, or rescind suitable procedural regulations to carry out the provisions of this title. Regulations issued under this section shall be in conformity with the standards and limitations of the Administrative Procedure Act.

60 Stat. 237. 5 USC 1001 note.

(b) In any action or proceeding based on any alleged unlawful employment practice, no person shall be subject to any liability or punishment for or on account of (1) the commission by such person of an unlawful employment practice if he pleads and proves that the act or omission complained of was in good faith, in conformity with, and in reliance on any written interpretation or opinion of the Commission, or (2) the failure of such person to publish and file any information required by any provision of this title if he pleads and proves that he failed to publish and file such information in good faith, in conformity with the instructions of the Commission issued under this title regarding the filing of such information. Such a defense, if established, shall be a bar to the action or proceeding, notwithstanding that (A) after such act or omission, such interpretation or opinion is modified or rescinded or is determined by judicial authority to be invalid or of no legal effect, or (B) after publishing or filing the description and annual reports, such publication or filing is determined by judicial authority not to be in conformity with the requirements of this title.

FORCIBLY RESISTING THE COMMISSION OR ITS REPRESENTATIVES

SEC. 714. The provisions of section 111, title 18, United States Code, shall apply to officers, agents, and employees of the Commission in the performance of their official duties.

62 Stat. 688.

SPECIAL STUDY BY SECRETARY OF LABOR

SEC. 715. The Secretary of Labor shall make a full and complete study of the factors which might tend to result in discrimination in employment because of age and of the consequences of such discrimination on the economy and individuals affected. The Secretary of Labor shall make a report to the Congress not later than June 30, 1965, containing the results of such study and shall include in such report such recommendations for legislation to prevent arbitrary discrimination in employment because of age as he determines advisable.

Report to Congress.

- 84

EFFECTIVE DATE

SEC. 716. (a) This title shall become effective one year after the date of its enactment.

(b) Notwithstanding subsection (a), sections of this title other than sections 703, 704, 706, and 707 shall become effective immediately.

Presidential conferences.

(c) The President shall, as soon as feasible after the enactment of this title, convene one or more conferences for the purpose of enabling the leaders of groups whose members will be affected by this title to become familiar with the rights afforded and obligations imposed by its provisions, and for the purpose of making plans which will result in the fair and effective administration of this title when all of its provisions become effective. The President shall invite the participation in such conference or conferences of (1) the members of the President's Committee on Equal Employment Opportunity, (2) the members of the Commission on Civil Rights, (3) representatives of State and local agencies engaged in furthering equal employment opportunity, (4) representatives of private agencies engaged in furthering equal employment opportunity, and (5) representatives of employers, labor organizations, and employment agencies who will be subject to this title.

Membership.

TITLE VIII—REGISTRATION AND VOTING STATISTICS

Survey.

SEC. 801. The Secretary of Commerce shall promptly conduct a survey to compile registration and voting statistics in such geographic areas as may be recommended by the Commission on Civil Rights. Such a survey and compilation shall, to the extent recommended by the Commission on Civil Rights, only include a count of persons of voting age by race, color, and national origin, and determination of the extent to which such persons are registered to vote, and have voted in any statewide primary or general election in which the Members of the United States House of Representatives are nominated or elected, since January 1, 1960. Such information shall also be collected and compiled in connection with the Nineteenth Decennial Census, and at such other times as the Congress may prescribe. The provisions of section 9 and chapter 7 of title 13, United States Code, shall apply to any survey, collection, or compilation of registration and voting statistics carried out under this title: *Provided, however*, That no person shall be compelled to disclose his race, color, national origin, or questioned about his political party affiliation, how he voted, or the reasons therefore, nor shall any penalty be imposed for his failure or refusal to make such disclosure. Every person interrogated orally, by written survey or questionnaire or by any other means with respect to such information shall be fully advised with respect to his right to fail or refuse to furnish such information.

68 Stat. 1013, 1022; 76 Stat. 922. 13 USC 9, 211-241.

TITLE IX—INTERVENTION AND PROCEDURE AFTER REMOVAL IN CIVIL RIGHTS CASES

63 Stat. 102.

SEC. 901. Title 28 of the United States Code, section 1447(d), is amended to read as follows:

"An order remanding a case to the State court from which it was removed is not reviewable on appeal or otherwise, except that an order remanding a case to the State court from which it was removed pursuant to section 1443 of this title shall be reviewable by appeal or otherwise."

62 Stat. 938.

SEC. 902. Whenever an action has been commenced in any court of the United States seeking relief from the denial of equal protection of the laws under the fourteenth amendment to the Constitution on ac-

85

count of race, color, religion, or national origin, the Attorney General for or in the name of the United States may intervene in such action upon timely application if the Attorney General certifies that the case is of general public importance. In such action the United States shall be entitled to the same relief as if it had instituted the action.

TITLE X—ESTABLISHMENT OF COMMUNITY RELATIONS SERVICE

SEC. 1001. (a) There is hereby established in and as a part of the Department of Commerce a Community Relations Service (hereinafter referred to as the "Service"), which shall be headed by a Director who shall be appointed by the President with the advice and consent of the Senate for a term of four years. The Director is authorized to appoint, subject to the civil service laws and regulations, such other personnel as may be necessary to enable the Service to carry out its functions and duties, and to fix their compensation in accordance with the Classification Act of 1949, as amended. The Director is further authorized to procure services as authorized by section 15 of the Act of August 2, 1946 (60 Stat. 810; 5 U.S.C. 55(a)), but at rates for individuals not in excess of $75 per diem.

Post, p. 400. 5 USC 1071 note.

(b) Section 106(a) of the Federal Executive Pay Act of 1956, as amended (5 U.S.C. 2205(a)), is further amended by adding the following clause thereto:

70 Stat. 737.

"(52) Director, Community Relations Service."

Functions.

SEC. 1002. It shall be the function of the Service to provide assistance to communities and persons therein in resolving disputes, disagreements, or difficulties relating to discriminatory practices based on race, color, or national origin which impair the rights of persons in such communities under the Constitution or laws of the United States or which affect or may affect interstate commerce. The Service may offer its services in cases of such disputes, disagreements, or difficulties whenever, in its judgment, peaceful relations among the citizens of the community involved are threatened thereby, and it may offer its services either upon its own motion or upon the request of an appropriate State or local official or other interested person.

SEC. 1003. (a) The Service shall, whenever possible, in performing its functions, seek and utilize the cooperation of appropriate State or local, public, or private agencies.

(b) The activities of all officers and employees of the Service in providing conciliation assistance shall be conducted in confidence and without publicity, and the Service shall hold confidential any information acquired in the regular performance of its duties upon the understanding that it would be so held. No officer or employee of the Service shall engage in the performance of investigative or prosecuting functions of any department or agency in any litigation arising out of a dispute in which he acted on behalf of the Service. Any officer or other employee of the Service, who shall make public in any manner whatever any information in violation of this subsection, shall be deemed guilty of a misdemeanor and, upon conviction thereof, shall be fined not more than $1,000 or imprisoned not more than one year.

Report to Congress.

SEC. 1004. Subject to the provisions of sections 205 and 1003(b), the Director shall, on or before January 31 of each year, submit to the Congress a report of the activities of the Service during the preceding fiscal year.

86

TITLE XI—MISCELLANEOUS

Trial by jury.

SEC. 1101. In any proceeding for criminal contempt arising under title II, III, IV, V, VI, or VII of this Act, the accused, upon demand therefor, shall be entitled to a trial by jury, which shall conform as near as may be to the practice in criminal cases. Upon conviction, the accused shall not be fined more than $1,000 or imprisoned for more than six months.

Exceptions.

This section shall not apply to contempts committed in the presence of the court, or so near thereto as to obstruct the administration of justice, nor to the misbehavior, misconduct, or disobedience of any officer of the court in respect to writs, orders, or process of the court. No person shall be convicted of criminal contempt hereunder unless the act or omission constituting such contempt shall have been intentional, as required in other cases of criminal contempt.

Nor shall anything herein be construed to deprive courts of their power, by civil contempt proceedings, without a jury, to secure compliance with or to prevent obstruction of, as distinguished from punishment for violations of, any lawful writ, process, order, rule, decree, or command of the court in accordance with the prevailing usages of law and equity, including the power of detention.

Double jeopardy.

SEC. 1102. No person should be put twice in jeopardy under the laws of the United States for the same act or omission. For this reason, an acquittal or conviction in a prosecution for a specific crime under the laws of the United States shall bar a proceeding for criminal contempt, which is based upon the same act or omission and which arises under the provisions of this Act; and an acquittal or conviction in a proceeding for criminal contempt, which arises under the provisions of this Act, shall bar a prosecution for a specific crime under the laws of the United States based upon the same act or omission.

Attorney General, etc., authority.

SEC. 1103. Nothing in this Act shall be construed to deny, impair, or otherwise affect any right or authority of the Attorney General or of the United States or any agency or officer thereof under existing law to institute or intervene in any action or proceeding.

States' authority.

SEC. 1104. Nothing contained in any title of this Act shall be construed as indicating an intent on the part of Congress to occupy the field in which any such title operates to the exclusion of State laws on the same subject matter, nor shall any provision of this Act be construed as invalidating any provision of State law unless such provision is inconsistent with any of the purposes of this Act, or any provision thereof.

Appropriation.

SEC. 1105. There are hereby authorized to be appropriated such sums as are necessary to carry out the provisions of this Act.

Separability clause.

SEC. 1106. If any provision of this Act or the application thereof to any person or circumstances is held invalid, the remainder of the Act and the application of the provision to other persons not similarly situated or to other circumstances shall not be affected thereby.

Approved July 2, 1964.

817

기 안 용 지

분류기호 문서번호	미이	(전화번호)	전결규정 조 항 장관 전결사항
처리기간		후열	
시행일자			
보존년한		차 관	장 관

보조기관			협조
	차관보		
	구미국장		
	북미2과장		
기안책임자	박양천	북미2과 (71. 9. 6.)	

경유 수신 참조	건 의	발신		통제	

제목: 군, 민관계 임시분과위원회 위원 위촉

최근 주한미군 기지촌 거주 한국인 주민과 미군인간의 빈번한 충돌 사건을 방지하기 위하여 한.미 합동위원회 실무 기관으로 "군, 민관계 임시 분과위원회"를 설치하고자 정부 관계부처에 위원 추천을 의뢰하였든 바, 관계부처로 부터 해당 위원의 추천이 있아옵기 다음과 같이 위원 위촉하여 표기 분과위원회 한국측 대표단을 구성할 것을 건의 합니다.

- 다 음 -

위원장	외무부	구미국	북미 2과장	외무부이사관	김형근
간 사	"		북미 2과	외무서기관	김기조
위 원	내무부	치안국	외사과장	경무관	김봉균
위 원	"		외사과	총 경	이병모
위 원	"	지방국	관리과장	행정서기관	백세현
위 원	법무부	법무실	송무과	검 사	정구영
위 원	"	검찰국	검찰과	검 사	현홍주
위 원	교통부	관광국	진흥과장	행정서기관	김철용

정서 / 관인 / 발송

공통서식 1—2 (갑)
1967. 4. 4 승인

190mm×268mm 중질지 7 g/m²
조달청 1,000,000매 인쇄)

88

위 원 보사부 (~~주무위촉~~) 고호 [illegible]
보건국 만성병담당관실 사무관

참고로 미측 명단을 첨부함.

첨부 : 미국측 위원 명단 1 부.

89

US Component

Ad Hoc Subcommittee on Civil-Military Relations

Captain Frank M. Romanick, USN, J5	Chairman
Colonel D. P. Heekin, USA, DCS, EUSA	Member
Colonel R. G. Eklund, USAF, Vice Commander, 314th Air Division	Member
Colonel B. T. Coggins, USA, JAJ	Member
Colonel J. K. Pope, USA, Surgeon	Member
Colonel R. J. Kriwanek, USA, Provost Marshal	Member
Mr. John P. Leonard, US Embassy	Member
Mr. Robert A. Kinney, USFK, J5	Secretary

90

공 란

공 란

공 란

공 란

공　　란

공 란

二

외 무 부

71 년 9 월 7 일

보건사회부 보건국장 전화 (11:30시)

하기 직원을 Ad hoc Subcommittee 의 member 로 해주시기 바람.

기.

고효균 사무관

Ko Hyo Kyun

보건국. 만성병 담당관실

Chronic disease control section.
Public Health Bureau
Min. of Public Health & Social Affairs.

917

구 미 국 장

공 란

공 란

공 란

공　란

공 란

공　　　란

공 란

공 란

공 란

공 란

공 

공 란

공 란

공 란

공 란

공 란

공 란

Body Set for GI-Korean Problems

71.9.8.K.T.

The ROK-U.S. Status of Forces Agreement joint committee yesterday established an ad hoc subcommittee on civil-military relations to investigate and analyze problems involving U.S. military personnel and Koreans living near or working in U.S. military installations.

The committee will make recommendations to the joint committee for necessary action designed to eliminate conditions which would adversely affect Korea-U.S. relations, and to promote continued mutual understanding and harmonious ties between the Korean people and U.S. servicemen.

Kim Hyung-kun, chief of the North American second section of the Foreign Ministry, was appointed as the Korean chairman of the subcommittee.

The subcommittee held its first meeting at the Capitol yesterday and made plans for information gathering trips to various U.S. bases and adjacent Korean communities, beginning Friday.

← 1971. 9. 8 Korea Times

韓美軍民關係分委발족

基地村불상사해결

71.9.8 동아

미군기지촌주변에서 일어나고 있는 한국인과 미군사이의 불상사를 해결키위해 韓美合同委員會아래 「軍民關係 임시분과위원회」가 발족, 七日 외무부에서 첫회의를 열었다。

← 1971. 9. 8 동아일보

115

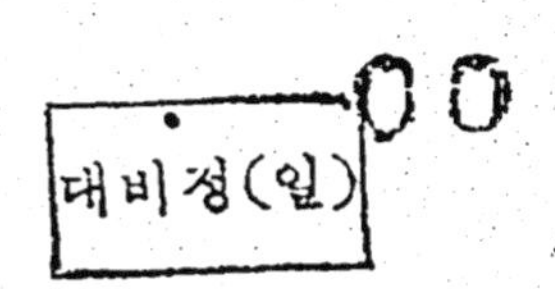

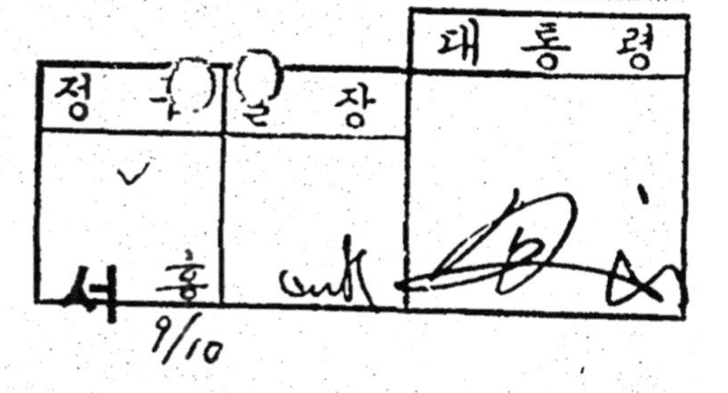

보 고 서

정 무

보고번호 제 71-594호

1971. 9. 9.

문서분류번호	보존기간
700	영구(가)

대통령 각하

보고관 오 명

제 목: 한국민간인과 주한 미군간의 충돌 재발 방지를 위한 조치 (외무부보고)

보 고 요 지 :

7.9 평택에서 발생한 흑인병사와 현지주민간의 충돌사건 및 8. 18 동두천 주민 150명과 미군헌병 80명간의 투석전등 한국민간인과 미국군인간의 충돌사건에 대하여,

가. 미국내 신문들이 동 충돌사건의 원인을 "흑인에 대한 한국인의 인종차별에서 기인한다"고 보도함으로써, 미국 흑인 하원의원들은 한국인의 흑인 차별대우를 비난, 한국에 대한 미국의 원조 중단을 주장한바 있으며,

나. "언더힐"주한미공사는 9.1 외무장관에게 흑인 하원의원들의 흑백 차별대우 근절을 요청하는 "닉슨"대통령앞 연판장과 "로저스"국무장관이 미군주둔 전재외공관에게 흑백 차별대우 해소를 위하여 가능한 조치를 취하라고 지시한 문서를 제시하고, 한국정부의 가능한 조치와 협조를 요청하였는바,

충돌사건의 원인, 영향판단 및 사건 재발 방지를 위한 조치내용을 다음과 같이 보고드립니다.

대 통 령 비 서 실

3-1

116

1. 충돌사건의 원인 :

가. 미군측 주장 :

(1) 흑백병사가 출입하는 클럽이 각각 구분되어 있음.

(2) 일부 클럽에서는 업주, 종업원이 흑인을 차별대우함.

(3) 미군기지 주변 지역 한국관헌의 통제 및 대미협조가 미온적임.

나. 한국측 주장 :

(1) 흑백클럽의 구분은 미군 자신들의 선택의 결과임.

(2) 흑인에 대한 차별은 백인병사의 흑인에 대한 인종의식의 반영에 불과함.

(3) 숫자적으로 적은 흑인은 소비가 적은 반면, 일반적으로 포악함.(백인 : 흑인 = 10 : 1)

2. 충돌사건이 미치는 영향 판단 :

가. 충돌사건의 재발은 인종문제와 결부되어 미국 흑인의원들을 자극, 미국의 대한국정책에 불리한 압력으로 나타날 것이며, 특히 해외주재 미군의 철수를 요구하는 미국내 여론이 고조되고 있는 현시점에서 한.미관계 전반에 좋지않은 영향을 미칠 우려가 있음.

나. 충돌사건이 정치문제화됨으로써 주한미군 당국은 사건의 예방을 위하여 강경조치를 불사하고 있는바, 사건발생 지역에 대한 미군의 출입금지명등은 기지 주변 주민의 생계를 위협하고 있음.

대 통 령 비 서 실

3 - 2

117

00 00

3. 충돌사건 재발 방지를 위한 조치 내용 :

가. 한국정부의 조치 :

(1) 미국정부, 의회 및 언론기관에 사건의 진상을 설명하고, 한국인은 민족적 차별의식이 없는 점등을 홍보함.

(2) 관계부처 (외무, 내무, 법무, 보사, 서울시, 관광협회) 간의 협의를 통하여 충돌사건 방지책을 강구함.

나. 주한미군당국의 조치 :

(1) 사건기지 미군의 외출을 금지함.

(2) 이태원 접객업자들에게 흑백차별을 하지 않겠다는 서약서를 받음.

다. 한.미합동위원회의 조치 :

충돌사건의 근본적문제를 해결하기 위하여 9. 2 "군, 민 관계 임시분과위원회"를 설치키로 합의함.

(1) 구성 : 외무, 내무, 법무, 교통, 보사부의 관계관을 한국측 위원으로 임촉.

(2) 기능 : 주한미군과 기지주변 주민간의 문제뿐만아니라 미군부대 근무 한국인 종업원과 미군간의 제문제의 실태를 조사, 파악하고 해결책을 한.미 합동위원회에 건의.

유 첨 : 1. 한국 민간인과 미국 군인간의 충돌사건 방지대책. (외무부 보고 71. 9. 6)

2. 평택사건에 대한 처리결과 보고.(외무부 보고 71. 7. 26)

끝

대 통 령 비 서 실
3 - 3

118

Ad Hoc Subcommittee on Civil-Military Relations

Trip to Camp Casey - Tongduchon

Friday, 10 September 1971

0930	Depart from H-201, Yongsan Helipad.
1000-1030	Arrive at Camp Casey. Greetings from MG G. H. Woodward, Commander, US 2d Division.
1030-1230	Discussion with ROK Officials in Tongduchon.
1245-1330	Lunch at Camp Casey.
1330-1530	Discussion with US military authorities at Camp Casey.
1530-1615	Tour of Tongduchon. Time of tour of Tongduchon is flexible, depending upon length of discussions. Part of tour could be held before lunch and part just before departure from Camp Casey in the afternoon.
1615-1630	Depart from Camp Casey - R-220.
1630-1700	Arrive H-201, Yongsan Helipad.

119

현지 참석 범위 (15 명)

양주 군수	민 충 근
의정부 경찰시장	고 인 준
동두천 읍장	지 덕 운
동두천 지서장	조 동 수
관광협회 동두천 지부장	이 건 차
" 총무	이 창 우
보건 지소장	박 규
제1 성병 관리소장	이 인 숙
제 2 "	임 병 문
제 3 "	김 봉 덕
제5 "	유 종 린
민들레 총회장	김 상 수
" 감찰	이 송 자
" 감찰	이 정 화
" 감찰	이 금 순

120

공 

공 란

한국관광휴양업협회 양주지부

요망사항 Tourism entertainment Assoc 1971. 9. 10.

고통산하

1. 보건위생

(1) 위생시설 관리방법 월1회 검열

우리관광휴양업소는 정부의 위생시설 규정에 의하여 허가를 득하고 있으며 매월마다 정기적으로 검열을 받으며 시설개선에 노력하고 있다.

(2) 성병관리

ㄱ. 원인

성병전염은 검진증이 없는 업태부와의 접촉하는데 그원인이 있음

ㄴ. 대책

검진증(합격된 자) 소지자에 한하여 접촉할 것이며 그외에 노상청객, 영내 및 기타장소에서 접촉을 금지할것.

숙녀

(3) 마약및 환각제 관계

일정하게 지정된 장소 이외의 출입을 금지시킬것.

2. P.X. 물품 유출.

(1) 원인

외출시 필요이상의 물품휴대를 허용하고 있음.

예로서 1970년도에는 맥주 6켄이 허용한데 비해 지난달까지 1박스(24켄)까 허용되

123

였고 군간에는 반박스(12켄)씩 휴대하고 있으며 외출회수에 제한이 없음으로 다량의켄맥주가 유출되고 있음.

(2) 대책

외출시에는 P.X. 물품및 군용품을 일체 휴대치 못하게 할것.

3. 흑백 분규

우리 업자로서는 흑.백인이 다 고객이므로 평등하게 친절과 봉사를 다하고 있으나 미군 흑.백인간에 인종차별에 기인함. customers

예로서 흑인을 상대한 업태부는 백인으로 부터 경원을 당하고 있기때문에 그 나마의 직업을 잃게 된다. 미군안에 있다.

4. 결론

(1). 미군들의 출입처를 지정하고 지정장소 이외에는 출입을 금지시켜야 된다. 성병, 마약,

(2). 외출시의 물품휴대를 금지시킨다.

마약 도매상 — 미국에 mail

124

마약

대매

Ad Hoc Subcommittee on Civil-Military Relations

Trip to Camp Humphreys - Anjong-ni

Monday, 13 September 1971

0930	Depart from H-201, Yongsan Helipad
1000-1010	Arrive at Camp Humphreys.
1010-1230	Discussion with ROK officials from Pyongtaek and Anjong-ni at Paing Sung Myon Office.
1245-1330	Lunch at Camp Humphreys.
1330-1530	Discussion with US military authorities at Camp Humphreys.
1530-1615	Tour of Anjong-ni.
1615-1630	Depart from Camp Humphreys.
16[illegible]5-1700	Arrive H-201, Yongsan, Helipad.

125

ITINERARY SOFA JOINT COMMITTEE

0930	Depart Yongsan by helicopter
0950	Arrive H-220
0950-1000	Debark; introductions
1000-1015	Travel by bus to Div HQ Conference room and introductions
1015-1030	Greeting remarks by Commanding General
1030-1040	Travel to Tongduchon. Guides and itinerary provided by Korean representatives.
1040-1235	Briefings and tour by local officials
1235-1245	Travel from TDC to Krueger Hall
1245-1330	Lunch at Krueger Hall
1330-1335	Travel to Div HQ Conference room
1335-1530	Briefings by selected Division Staff Officers
1530-1630	Tour of TDC conducted by G-5
1630	Depart H220

126

Korean News Round-up 10 Sept. 1971

GUARD SHOOTING INCIDENT FALSE Hankuk Ilbo/DNA (9 September)

A report that an American soldier allegedly shot to death an unidentified person while on duty turned out to be false Wednesday, the Hankuk Ilbo reported Thursday morning.

Private First Class Rebrang (phonetic), 25, of a US Army missile unit near Ansong, Kyonggi Province had been sought on a tip from a GI that he had opened fire on an unidentified man approaching his compound while on duty in the afternoon of Aug. 30.

Private First Class Rebrang was found to have falsely told his comrade, Corporal Runa (phonetic) that he had shot a man to death when actually he shot at a warning sign in front of the unit compound. The GI is alleged to be a drunkard and narcotic addict who smokes "happy smokes."

A US military investigation team which had been requested by Ansong police to cooperate in finding the "body of the victim" and arresting the suspect, had searched for a week for the GI. Rebrang has been confined to his unit's stockade on a charge of violence while under heavy alcoholic influence, the report said.

PYONGTAEK BUSINESS STILL DOWN DESPITE BAN LIFT Kyonggi Ilbo/HAP(9 September)

Economic activities are still dull in local communities, although the 28th US Support Command lifted an off-limits order on its personnel Aug. 26, 48 days after the riot involving Negro soldiers.

The reason is that although the ban has been lifted, a limited number of soldiers were allowed to leave their camp in order to prevent the reoccurance of riot.

Since there are only a few GIs going outside, only four of the nine GI entertainment halls are now in operation in the area.

The local Korean community welcomed the lifting of the off-limits ban. However, they are still dissatisfied with US Army authorities because only a few soldiers were allowed to leave their camp at a time.

In addition, various problems, including compensation for damaged furniture and equipment and the aggravated sentiments between U.S. military personnel and villagers, remain unsolved.

Meanwhile, Army authorities and the local Korean police strengthened a joint mobile patrol in the area to prevent trouble.

Pertinent 13 Sept Trip

14 25
6 7

40% YANGJU CAMP GIRLS UNDER 20 Chosun Ilbo/DNA (9 September)

Some 40 percent of the 1,600 camp followers residing in the vicinity of Yangju proved to be under the age of 20, the Yangju County Health Center revealed.

In a dispatch from Tongduchon, the Chosun Ilbo said Thursday that some 650 of a total of 1,600 camp-side girls scattered in six different places in Yangju County are under the age of 20 years old, and 400 of those were issued health certificates by cheating on their ages. A girl below 20 years of age is not eligible to have such certificate.

The rate of venereal disease germ carriage by those under 20 years old has increased by 6 percent over the previous year, the paper added.

The Yangju County authorities designated 21 days starting today through the end of this month as "return home period" for the camp followers and decided to make positive efforts to control the girls.

Pertinent 10 Sept Trip

ASSEMBLED BY THE EIGHTH U.S. ARMY PUBLIC AFFAIRS OFFICE
COMMAND INFORMATION DIVISION. TEL: YONGSAN 3216

127 Incl 7

MY DEAR FRIENDS

I AM VERY HAPPY TO HAVE A GRAND OPENING ON MAY 20TH OF THE STAR CLUB FOR UN PERSONNEL 6 PM

I WOULD LIKE TO ASK YOUR VISITS. AS YOU ARE WELL AWARE THERE IS NO CLUB THAT HAS HAD PROFESSIONAL SOUL MUSIC.

NOW I HASTEN TO INFORM YOU THAT THIS CLUB BRINGS YOU SATISFACTION. WE SHALL EXTEND OUR UTMOST TO HAVE YOUR DRINKING ATMOSPHERE JOVIAL AND HILARIOUS WITH GOOD LOOKING BAR MAIDS AND ENCHANTING MUSIC.

PLEASE MAKE THIS CLUB YOURS

THANK YOU

TRULY YOURS

KIM TAE PIL

OWNER OF CLUB

STAR CLUB

- LOCATION -

MAIN GATE

KO-RYO STORE

OB CLUB

PARADICE

BLACKS

STAR CLUB

업주로부터 직접 ~~ 되어
배포되었음.

128

보 건 사 회 부

보 건 1430-15753 1971. 9. 10

수 신 외무부장관

제 목 한국인과 미군인간의 충돌사건 방지대책 위원 추천

1. 미이 723-17981 (1971.9.1)관련임.
2. 당부 "군민 관계 임시분과위원회" 위원을 다음과 같이 추천 합니다.

직 위	성 명
보건관리관	민창동.

끝

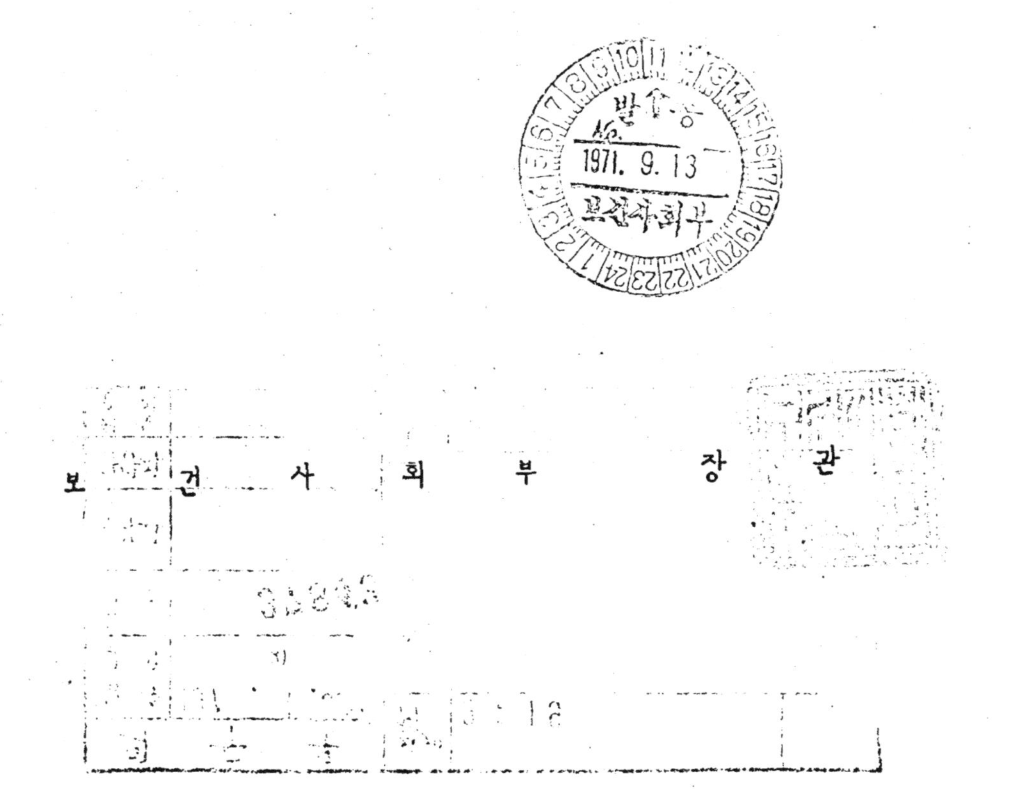

보 건 사 회 부 장 관

129

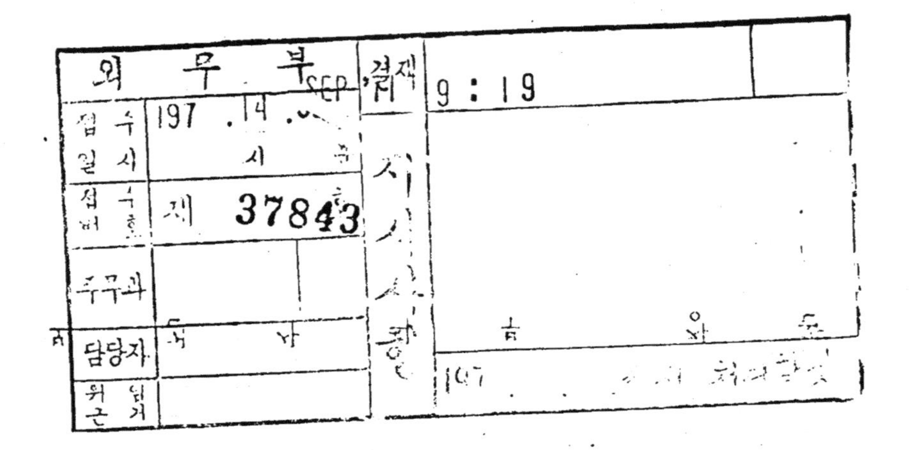

보 건 사 회 부

보건 1430-15753 1971. 9. 10

수신 외무부장관

제목 한국인과 미국인간의 충돌사건 방지대책 위원 추천

1. 미이 723-17981 (1971.9.1)관련임.
2. 당부 "군민관계 임시분과위원회" 위원을 다음과 같이 추천합니다.

직 위	성 명
보건관리관	민 장 홍.

끝

JOINT COMMITTEE
UNDER
THE REPUBLIC OF KOREA AND THE UNITED STATES
STATUS OF FORCES AGREEMENT

15 September 1971

Dear Gen. Smith,

In reference with my letter of 7 September 1971, I would like to imform you that Mr. MIN Chang Dong, Public Health Control Officer, Ministry of Health and Social Affairs (Tel. 75-6881) is appointed to replace Mr. KO Hyo Kyun as a member of the ROK component of the Ad Hoc Subcommittee on Civil-Military Relations.

Sincerely,

Koo Choong Whay
Republic of Korea
Representative

Lt Gen Robert N. Smith
United States Air Force
United States Representative

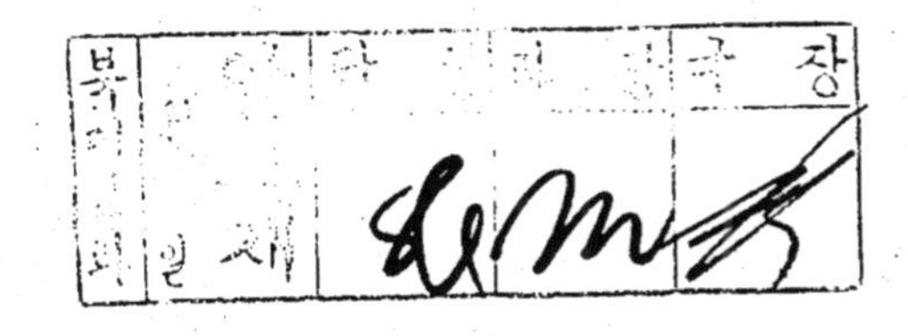

-130

면 담 요 록

1. 면 담 자 : 구미국 북미 2과장 김혁근, 김기조 서기관
   미 8군 J-5 SOFA 미측 간사 R. Kinney

2. 일 시 : 1971. 9. 14. 11:20 - 11:50

3. 면담요지 :

김 과장 - 동두천에서 1971. 9. 13. 저녁 오아시스 및 뉴.코리아 접객업소에게 내린 미 2사단측의 금족령은 증거도 없고 사전통고 및 교정조치의 여유도 없는 일방적 처사인바, 그러한 조치는 한.미 군민 분과위원회가 현지를 방문한지 3일 만에 취하여진 것으로 이는 한.미 양측의 노력을 멸시하는 일방적이며 비협조적인 조치이므로 즉시 금족령을 철회할 것을 요청하였으며, 조속한 시일내에 해결되지 않는다면 분과위원회 활동을 정지하겠다. 데모가 일어날 가능성이 있으니 유념하여야 할 것이다.

Kinney - 이 사건의 연락을 받았는 바, 한국측 제시와 동일하지는 않지만 즉시 조사하여 적절한 조치를 취하겠다. 군민 분과위 활동 정지는 미측 조치 진행을 기다려 주기 바란다.

121

주후의 전화 연락 : 현재 명령 계통을 통하여
조사중이며, 조치를 취하려 하고 있다. 데모와
같은 사태가 일어나지 않도록 조치하여 주기 바란다.

132

면 담 요 록

1. 면 담 자 : 구미국 북미 2과장 김형근, 김기조 서기관
주한 미대사관 정무과 Leonard 서기관

2. 일 시 : 1971. 9. 14. 14:30 - 15:00

3. 면담요지 :

김 과장 - Kinney 에 대한 presentation 과 동일. (추가하여) 이 presentation 을 Underhill 공사(이 문제에 직접 책임지고 있으므로)에게 보고하고 적절한 조치를 취하기 바란다.

Leonard - 조사하고 위에 보고하여 적절한 조치를 취하도록 하겠다. 연이나 분과위 활동을 정지할 필요는 없다고 보며, 이러한 사건을 예로들어 분과위가 교정하도록 노력하여야 할 것이다. 동두천에서 민심이 악화되고 있다면 큰 문제이다.

133

회 담 요 록

1. 방문자명 : 동두천 한국 관광휴양업협회 양주지부장 이건자 외 1 명 (동 총무)

2. 일 시 : 1971. 7. 14. 10:00 - 11:00

3. 면담자 : 김형근 북미 2과장, 김기조 서기관

4. 면담요지 :

방문자들은 미 2사단 사령부측에서 1971. 7. 13.밤을 기하여 동두천읍내 2개클럽 (오아시스, 뉴.코리아)에게 무기한 미군인 출입 금지령을 내렸는 바, 그 이유는 9. 11. 오아시스에서는 흑인 차별대우 (접대부의 춤 거절), 뉴.코리아에서는 위생불결 (어름 사용) 이었다 함. 양 업소는 그러한 사실을 극력 부인하고 있으며 사단 사령부측으로부터 사전 통고가 없었다 함.

관광협회측은 7. 13. 하오 2시 30분 확실한 증거도 없을 뿐만 아니라 사전통고나 교정을 위한 사전 유예기간도 주지않고 취한 미측의 일방적인 조치에 항의하였다 함. 이러한 미측의 불법조치를 교정하여 주기를 바람.

9.18. 뉴코리아 〉 각기 금족령이 해제됨
9.20. 오아시스

134

1. 業所 出入禁止 問題 (1~2頁)
2. 韓美間의 事故 問題 (3頁)
3. 오아시스 및 뉴-코리안 出入禁止 (4頁)
4. 美工師團長사관으로 [illegible] [illegible] (5.6.7頁)

※ 參考綴

1. 한미친선 관계 철
2. 한미 사고 철

한국관광휴양업협회[illegible]주지부

135

業所 出入禁止 問題

過去美七師團 時에는 月例 韓美親善
會와 風紀團束委員會를 通하여 事前
連絡 是正(레지) 指導하고 不得已 한 境
遇 出入禁止를 斷行 한바 있으나
美二師團 駐屯以后 부터는 모든 節
次를 무시 하고 美人 들의 一方的
橫暴를 방자 어느때 어떻게 누가 차
별 대우 했다는 根거도 없이 어느때 부
터 出入禁止 라는 通告만으로 不法斷
行 하고 있음을 너무나도 억울 함
은 勿論 우리 들의 主權마자 박탈
하는 處사 임을 痛感 합니다
그 實例를 別紙와 如히 열거 하면
서 이런 不法處事를 時急히 是正 하여
주시기 바라는 마음 간절 합니다

136

1. 1971年 6月 30日 下午 5時를 期하여 同年 7月 5日까지 地域的으로, 히피스모크 등 우범地대라는 理由로서, 無條件 한강정·성광·몬타나·아자무 4個 業所가 出入禁止를 當하였음

2. 1971年 7月 21日부터 同年 7月 24日까지 한강정 홀을 흑인 차별 대우를 했다는 理由로 (根거가 없음) 出入禁止 措置 하였음

3. 1971年 3月 13日 1日間 美軍들끼리 홀에서 싸웠다고 一方的으로 出入禁止 措置를 하였음.
(確認된 業所 뉴 - 서울 홀)

4. 1971年 8月 19日 美軍들의 횡포로서 싸움을 했다고 全体 8個 業所(문제 確認된 業所)에 出入禁止 措置 하였음

137

韓美間의 事故 問題

1. 71年 3月 28日 21時 40分, 東豆川邑 保山里 491번지 (ORION)홀에서 미2사단 將兵의 흑인병사 3名 백인병 15명 等이 싸움이 나서, 홀內에 기물 10余만원을 부수고, 主人 및 종업원에 폭행을 가한 事實이 있었음

2. 71年 3月 29日 4時경 身分을 밝히지 않고 흑인 將校 1名(大尉) 士兵 大 5명이 위생 검열 및 甚한 行為를 [illegible] 하여 왔음, 이날 이런 方法으로 아래와 같이 홀마다 다니면서 횡포를 자행하였음
대검 · 뉴-욕 · 럭키 · 오아시스 · 뉴-코리아 · 한강정 · 몬타나 · 야자수 · 센트랄 · 성광홀 等임

3. 이밖에도 M.P 및 C.P가 巡察하면서 便所 및 홀바닥 [illegible] 等에 來日부터 出入禁止 시킨다는 等 횡포를 일삼아, 不安을 느끼게 한다

.138

3. 오아시스 및 뉴-코리아, 出入禁止
1971年 9月 13日 午後 營業時間을 期해
無期限 出入禁止 措置를 하고 있다
그 內容을 보면, 9月 11日 午前 오아시스클럽
支配人을 民사처로 出頭시켜, OASIS
홀에서는 女子가 흑인이 춤을 추자면, 안
추고 퇴하는 일이 있으니 注意하라 고
하고. 뉴-코리아 에는 어름을 쓰지 말
것을 指示주고 그날 저녁에 黑人士兵
이 오아시스클럽에 다시 검열을 制裁로
하였다 면서, 女子가 춤을 추자 는
데 거절 하였으며 뉴-코리아에는 어름
을 달라고 하지 않었는데 어름을 주
며 使用하고 있다는 理由로 師團長
指示라고 民사참모 가 出入禁止 通告를
받으며 下午 2時 30分, 商協會 支部
長과 總務가 民사처에 出頭, 헌병대
許용엽 을 通해 아래와 같이, 陳
述 한바 있다 (要旨)
支部長 · 全體會員을 民사 참모 께서 民衆要
請하는바 出張中 못 하여 來去하다

139

4

民亦, 괜찮읍니다

民亦 : 뉴코리아 및 오아시스 홀이 아래와 같은 理由로 오늘부터 出入禁止 師團長 指示가 있어 알립니다

◎ 오아시스홀 : 女子가 흑인에게 춤을 거절하고 안추어주어 차별대우를 했다는 점

◎ 뉴-코리아 : 여관을 使用하였다는 點

主席 : 어떤 女子인지 알수없으나 그女子가 춤을 거절 했다고 해서 그 家게를 出入禁止 시킨다는것은 너무나 不當하다. 土曜日 9月11日 그런 行動을 않고 철저히 홀에서 계몽指導하고 있다

民사 참모 : 9月11日 午後 9時30分에 흑인 士兵 검열관이 돌아보고 또 10時~ 11時에 再次 가보니 차별대우. 춤을 거절 하였다고 報告 되어있기 師團長 指示이니 할수 없다

總무 : 지난 7월20日 下午 5時, 민사참모 헌병참모, 의무참모, 물랑 지서장 보건소장 等 黑人士兵 座上 에서

40

앞으로 어떠한 일이 있드라도 事
前 連絡을 해서, 혼숙거절 한 女
子를 지적해서, 主人 또는 主婦人
에게 알리면, 主人이 當局에 措置
를 要請 해서 措置하기로 되였는
데 너무나 當局은 一方的인 不法
處事이며 앞으로 歸還向 判定이
困難하다

사장 : 本當에 假處를 주고 午後에 가
보서 그대로 하고 있다고 報告가 들
어왔다

主婦 ; 今般事態에 依한 處分가 즘
시 아쉬운 마음이다
今번에는 경고로 하고, 앞으로는 責任
지고 이런 일이 없도록 하겠다

사 : 師團長 指示이니 어찌 할 道
理가 없다

主婦 : 師團長을 만나게 해달라

사 : 오늘 바빠서 만날수 없다
그러므로 이번은 不可避하니 다음부터는
이런 일이 없도록 努力하겠다

141

支部長, 당신들은 흑인이 暴動 하는 대로 規制
制止도 안해보고 이런 要求를 하는
것은 너무나 不法이다
그리고 女子 한사람 때문에 事實
이있든 없든 그部隊에 出入禁止 시키
놓은 理解가 안간다
이번에는 當局이 알고 용서 해주
기 바란다
군사 : 우리로서는 表明 시킬수 없고, 來日
아침에 전화를 하겠으니 會議 이나
師團長에게 이야기 해보겠다

142

NON-DISCRIMINATION PLEDGE

무차별 대우 서약

I ________________, the Owner/Operator of the ________________,

본인 ________________ 은 ________________ 의 업주/운영자

recognise the absolute equality of all people, regardless of race, color

이며 인종, 색갈 또는 국적 여하를 막론하고 모든 사람은 절대적으로

or nationality, and pledge to do my utmost to insure equal treatment

평등함을 인식하며 이 모든 사람들에 대하여 동등한 대우를 다함을 서약

for all.

합니다.

I specifically pledge that should any of my employees discriminate

본인은 아울러 본인의 업소 내에서 나의 종업원들이 어떠한 차별 대우를

against any person on my premises, the offender will be discharged

여하한 사람에게도 하였을 때는 그 자는 즉시 나의 업소에서 해고

immediately from employment. Furthermore, should any business girl

시킬을 약속합니다. 이 이외도 어떠한 영업여자나 기타 다른

or other individual discriminate against any person on my premises,

분들의 사람들이 나의 업소에서 차별 대우를 하였을 때는 즉시 그 자를

the offender will be summarily removed and barred from reentering same.

퇴거시킴과 동시 차후 나의 업소에 다시 들어오지 못하도록 하겠읍니다.

I understand fully that, should I violate this pledge in any manner,

본인은 본인 자신이 여기 기재된 서약을 어떠한 형태로 위반 하였을 때는

I may expect that my premises will be placed "off-limits" to U.S.

나의 업소는 미군들의 "출입금지"를 당하게 됨을 충분히 인식하고

personnel.

있읍니다.

1. ________________

2. ________________

Owner/Operator of ________________

업주/운영자

Date: ________________

일 자:

143

DEPARTMENT OF THE ARMY
HEADQUARTERS 2D INFANTRY DIVISION
OFFICE OF THE ASSISTANT CHIEF OF STAFF, G5
APO SAN FRANCISCO 96224

EAIDGC 4 August 1971

SUBJECT: On-Limits Criteria for Clubs
제 목: 미군이 출입할수있는 크타브의 기준

TO: All Club Owners/Operators Servicing U.S. Personnel in the 2d Infantry Division Area
수신: 미제2사단 지역 내에서 미군 상대로 하는 전 크타브업주/영업자

1. The following criteria are the minimal sanitary practices required
다음에 기재된 기준은 미제2 보병사단 지역내에 있는 크타브들이
for clubs to obtain and maintain "on-limits" status in the 2d Infantry
"미군이 출입할수있는" 크타브로서 반듯이 구비되여 있어야할 최저한도의
Division area.
위생 기준입니다.

Doctor will check the glass-cups for determination using

a. Drinks will be served only in disposal paper cups; these will
음주는 반듯이 처분해 버릴수 있는 종이 잔에 한하여 사용하되 이
be used only one time and then disposed of.
잔의 사용은 단 한번만 사용하고 처분해야합니다.

b. Ice, unless tested and approved by the Division Surgeon, will
어름은 사단의무관이 실험하여 인정한 어름 이외는 여하한 음주에도
not be used in any drinks.
사용을 금합니다.

c. No food will be prepared or served in the club.
크타브 내에서는 음식 준비 또는 제공을 못 합니다.

d. There will be at least one functioning commode and urinal
한 크타브에 적어도 완전 사용 할수 있으며, 물이 흐르고 있는
and one wash basin with running water in each club; a bar of soap and
대소변기 및 한개의 세면대를 구비하여야하며, 여기에 비누 종이수건이
individual paper hand towels will be provided at the wash basin.
세면대에 구비되여 있어야 합니다.

144

EAIDGC 4 August 1971
SUBJECT: On-Limits Criteria for Clubs

e. The toilet area will be kept neat and clean.

화장실 지역은 잘 정비되며 깨끗이 되여 있어야 합니다.

f. The bar and lounge area will be kept neat and clean.

크타브의 바닥 및 빠 지역이 정돈되며 깨끗이 되여야 합니다.

g. Prices for all beverages will be posted behind the bar.

음료 가격표는 카운터 벽에 붙여 있어야 합니다.

2. Impartial and equal service must be given to all visitors regardless of race color or nationality.

인종, 색갈 또는 국적에 관계 없이 모든 손님에 대하여 공평하고 동등한 호의적인 대우를 하여야 합니다.

3. Any club which fails to meet the criteria listed above will be declared "off-limits" to U.S. personnel.

어떠한 크타브라도 상기한 기준과 합당하지 않을 때는 미군들에게 "출입금지"를 선언할 것 입니다.

OTTO N. RILEY, JR 오토. 엔. 라이리
LTC, GS 미중령
ACofS G5 민사참모

45

공 

공　　　　란

공　　　란

공　　　　란

Pt. Rogers talk. paper

Civil-military relations problems in Korea

Sometimes ago, I was informed of your instruction addressed to the U.S. chiefs of missions abroad concerning the problems between U.S. military personnel and the indigenous people.

With almost 40,000 U.S. troops stationed in its territory, Korea was not free of those problems. Since the question is a mutual concern of our two countries, my Government and the U.S. Forces in Korea have agreed to form a subcommittee under the Status of Forces Agreement Joint Committee specifically to deal with problems arising out of the contacts between U.S. soldiers and the Korean people.

However, the accusation of racism directed against Korean Government and Korean people by the so-called Black Caucus is totally unfounded. Historically, Korean people knows no racial segregation though they take a great pride in being a Korean, and cultural conflicts with foreigners never caused serious problems. In every society, there are incidents of discrimination against wrong-doings and bad behaviors. One can not call it a racial injustice because the discriminated wrong-doers happen to be a foreigner.

150

No one would benefit by such disturbances regardless of the causes. For this reason, the Korean Government is doing its best to prevent such incidents. At the same time, it should be understood that the facts are sometimes distorted or exagerated out of proportion to suit certain personal or political designs.

151

공 란

공 란

공

공 란

공 란

공　　란

공 란

공 란

공 란

공 란

공

공 란

기 안 용 지

분류기호 문서번호	미이 723 -	(전화번호)	전결규정 조 항 차관 전결사항
처리기간			
시행일자	71. 9. 23.		
보존년한		차 관	
보조기관	차관보		협조
	구미국장		
	북미 2과장		
기안책임자	김기조	북미 2과 (71. 9. 22)	
경유 수신 참조	문화공보부장관	발신	20350 1971. 9. 24 외무부 / 검열 1971. 9. 24 통제관
제 목	한국인과 미군인간의 충돌 사건 방지 대책		

1. 최근 주한미군의 기지주변에 거주하는 주민과 미군인간의 충돌 사건은 증가일로에 있는 바, 인종 차별 문제가 이러한 사건의 주요 원인으로 지적되므로써 미 의회와 행정부에서도 문제로 제기되고 있어 한.미 관계에 불리한 영향을 미칠 우려마저 없지않은 실정이었읍니다.

2. 이러한 불상사에 대한 대책을 마련하기 위하여 당부에서는 1971. 8. 18. 관계부처 실무자회의를 개최하였고, 한.미 합동위원회에서도 논의와 절충을 거듭한 끝에 별첨 각서에 따라 "군,민관계 임시 분과 위원회" (Ad Hoc Subcommittee on Civil-Military Relations) 를 합동위원회의 실무 기관으로 설치하기로 합의하고 이미 2차의 회의와 현지시찰을 실시한바 있읍니다.

3. 이에 따라 한국측에서는 외무, 내무, 법무, 교통및 보사부가 참여하고 있는 바, 문제의 성격과 앞으로 설치될 panel on people-to-people projects 의 운영을 위하여 귀부의 참여가 요청되오니

정서 / 관인 / 발송

공통서식 1-2 (갑)
1967. 4. 4 승인

190mm×268mm 중질지 7 g/m²
조 달 청 1,000,000매 인쇄)

164

관계과장을 동 분과위의 일원으로 지급 추천하여 주시기 바랍니다.

4. 참고로 본 분과위원회의 제1차 회의록, 합동위원회에 대한 제1차 보고서(특히 귀부 관련사항인 제3면의 g항 "대민관계 기획 패널"을 참조 바람)를 별첨 송부합니다.

첨부 : 1. 합동위원회 각서 1부.

2. 제1차 회의록.

3. 합동위원회에 대한 제1차 보고서. 끝

165.

외 무 부

미이 723 - (74 - 3073) 71. 9. 23.

수신 : 문화공보부장관

제목 : 한국인과 미군인간의 충돌사건 방지 대책

1. 최근 주한미군의 기지주변에 거주하는 주민과 미군인간의 충돌사건은 증가일로에 있는 바, 인종차별 문제가 이러한 사건의 주요 원인으로 지적되므로써 미 의회와 행정부에서도 문제로 제기되고 있어 한.미 관계에 불미한 영향을 미칠 우려마저 없지않은 실정이었읍니다.

2. 이러한 불상사에 대한 대책을 마련하기 위하여 당부에서는 1971. 8. 18. 관계부처 실무자회의를 개최하였고, 한.미 합동위원회에서도 논의와 절충을 거듭한 끝에 별첨 각서에 따라 "군,민관계 임시분과위원회" (Ad Hoc Subcommittee on Civil-Military Relations)를 합동위원회의 실무기관으로 설치하기로 합의하고 이미 2차의 회의와 현지시찰을 실시한바 있읍니다.

3. 이에 따라 한국측에서는 외무, 내무, 법무, 교통및 보사부가 참여하고 있는 바, 문제의 성격과 앞으로 설치될 panel on people-to-people projects 의 운영을 위하여 귀부의 참여가 요청되오니 관계과장을 동 분과위의 일원으로 지급 추천하여 주시기 바랍니다.

166

4. 참고로 본 분과위원회의 제1차 회의록, 합동위원회에 대한 제1차 보고서 (특히 귀부 관련사항인 제3면의 g 항 "대민관계 계획 제납" 을 참조 바람)를 별첨 송부합니다.

첨부 : (1) 합동위원회 공서 1부.

(2) 제1차 회의록.

(3) 합동위원회에 대한 제1차 보고서. 끝

외 무 부 장 관

167

정/리/보/존/문/서/목/록					
기록물종류	문서-일반공문서철	등록번호	510 4345	등록일자	
분류번호	729.419	국가코드		주제	
문서철명	SOFA 한.미국 합동위원회 군민관계 임시분과위원회, 제1-5차. 1971				
생산과	안보담당관실	생산년도	1971 ~ 1972	보존기간	영구
담당과(그룹)	미주	안보	서가번호	--	
참조분류					
권차명					
내용목차	1. 제1차. 1971.9.7 2. 제2차. 1971.9.22 3. 제3차. 1971.10.18 4. 제4차. 1971.11.19 5. 제5차. 1971.12.14				

마/이/크/로/필/름/사/항				
촬영연도	*롤 번호	화일 번호	후레임 번호	보관함 번호
2007-9-21	Re-07-09	8	1-213	

결 번

넘버링 오류

결번

넘버링 오류

I. 1차.

1971. 9. 7.

4

1

JOINT ROK-US PRESS RELEASE
SIXTY-FOURTH ROK-US JOINT COMMITTEE MEETING
29 JULY 1971

The ROK-US Joint Committee approved 27 recommendations of its Facilities and Areas Subcommittee and assigned 28 new tasks to the same Subcommittee at its sixty-fourth meeting, held on 29 July 1971 in the US SOFA Conference Room.

The Joint Committee approved the recommendation of its Finance (Personnel Affairs) Subcommittee, concerning revised procedures for examination of incoming APO parcel post packages by ROK customs inspectors. The Joint Committee also discussed the recent incidents involving US military personnel and Korean nationals which have taken place in the vicinity of some US military installations, with a view to forestalling recurrence of such incidents.

The next meeting of the ROK-US Joint Committee is scheduled to be held on Thursday, 26 August 1971.

대한민국 외무부
공보관실
전화 74-3576

보 도 자 료

이 기사는 제공처인 외무부를
밝히고 보도할수 있음

외무보도 호

년 월 일 시 분 발표

한.미 합동 위원회 제64차 회의
공 동 발 표 문

1971. 7. 29.

한.미 합동 위원회는 1971. 7. 29. 미측 회의실에서 제64차 회의를 개최하고 27건의 시설구역 분과위원회 건의를 승인하였으며, 28건의 과제를 동 분과위원회에 부여 하였다.

합동 위원회는 군사 우편(APO)소포 화물에 대한 한국 세관원의 검사 절차를 개정하는데 관한 재무 분과위원회 건의를 승인하였다.

합동 위원회는 또한 최근 일부 미군 시설 근처에서 한국인과 미군인간에 발생한 일련의 사건의 재발을 방지하는 방안을 토의하였다.

다음 한.미 합동 위원회 회의는 1971. 8. 26. 목요일에 개최될 예정이다.

6 71.10.3

주요 사건 일지

1. 7. 9 평택 난동 사건

흑인병사 약 50명이 인종 차별을 한다는 이유로 한국인이 경영하는 클럽에 난입, 850만원의 물적 피해와 한국인 8명에게 중경상을 입힘.

2. 7. 13 의정부 난동 사건

한국인이 미군 흑인과 위안부에게 야유를 하였다는 데서 발단, 미군 20여명과 주민 50여명이 투석전을 벌임.

3. 7. 16. 대전 위안부 데모 사건

위안부 100여명이 미군인의 위안부 살해사건을 항의하는 데모를 벌임.

4. 8. 2 왜관 데모 사건

미군의 한국인 구타 사건에 관련하여 주민 100여명과 미군인간에 난동이 벌어졌으나, 사상자는 발생하지 않았음.

5. 8. 9 평택 위안부 데모 사건

위안부 600여명과 주민이 금족령을 해제하라고 데모를 벌임.

주 요 사 건 일 지

1. 평택 난동 사건 (1971. 7. 9.)

7. 9. 21:00 경 평택 소재 미 제 23 직접지원단 미 흑인병사 약 50명은 한국인이 경영하는 일부 클럽이 흑인과 백인을 차별대우 한다는 데 불만을 품고 예고없이 이들 클럽에 난입, 한국인 1명에게는 중상을 입히고, 7명에게는 약 10일의 치료를 요하는 경상을 입혔으며, 853 만원 상당의 물적 피해를 가함. 이에 분격한 부락민 약 500 여 명은 난동 미군들을 비방하는 구호를 외치며, 미군 기지로 가다가 경찰관과 미 헌병의 제지로 해산됨.

2. 의정부 난동 사건 (1971. 7. 13.)

7. 13. 20:00 경 동두천읍 보산리 마을에서 미 제 2사단 소속 "로버트" 상병이 위안부와 동거중 한국인 18세 가량의 소년이 동 위안부를 야유, "로버트" 상병이 동 소년을 구타하려고 하는 것을 같은 마을에 거주하는 외상점이 제지하였는 바, 동 상병은 잠시후 동료 20여명과 같이 나타나 행패를 부리며 마자 주민 50여 명이 모여 상호 대치중 미 헌병대원 20여명이 출동, 이를 제지하면서 동 소년의 두부를 곤봉으로 강타, 전치 2주를 요하는 두부 타박상을 입힌바 있음.

8

3. 대전 위안부 데모 사건 (1971. 7. 16.)

위안부 김연숙과 미 833 병기중대 하사 "보비.존스"는 동거 중이었는 바, 7. 15. 밤부터 언쟁하다가 7. 16. 09:00 경 피해자가 반나체 변사체로 내실에서 발견되어 현지 경찰과 미 헌병대가 합동 수사한 결과, 가해자를 진범으로 단정, 검거하게 됨. 이에 격분한 약 100명의 위안부들은 동 살해사건을 항의하는 데모를 벌였음.

4. 왜관 사건 (1971. 8. 2.)

미군이 한국인을 구타한 사건이 발생하게 되자 현지 주민 다수와 미군인간에 난동이 벌어졌으나, 사상자는 발생하지 않았음.

5. 평택 데모 사건 (1971. 8. 9.)

접대부와 주민들이 7. 9. 사건과 관련된 미군의 금족령을 해제하라고 미군부대 앞에서 데모를 벌였음.

공 란

공 란

공 란

공 란

공 란

공 란

공 

공 란

공 란

공 란

공 란

공 란

공 란

공 란

공 

공 란

공 란

공 란

공 란

공 란

공 란

공 란

공 란

공 란

공 란

공 란

공 란

공 란

공 란

공 란

공 란

공 란

공 란

공 란

공 

공 란

공 란

공 란

공 란

공 란

공 란

공　　란

공 란

공 란

공 란

공 란

공 란

공 란

공 란

공 란

공 란

공　　　란

공 

공 란

공

공 란

공 란

공 란

공 란

공 란

공 란

공 란

공 란

공 란

공 란

공 란

공　　　란

공 란

공 란

공 

공　　　란

공 란

공 란

공 란

공 란

공　　　란

공

공 란

공

71. 10. 9 Stars & Stripes

Osan's EOT Officer

His Job Is Rocking the Boat

By S.SGT. C. E. WITTER
S&S Staff Writer

OSAN AB, Korea — The Equal Opportunity and Treatment (EOT) program here is, to some people, a radical idea, a system within a system to check the system. People from top to bottom can be shaken up by the program if they discriminate.

The man at Osan AB who admits that he rocks the boat is Capt. Tom Kroboth, the 314th Air Div. EOT officer.

Kroboth, an extrovert who loves to talk about his work, said that the "black and white problem is all over the world, and we have our share here.

"But you must remember," he continued, "it took centuries to create this problem and the answers are not found overnight."

Kroboth, who has had this full time job for seven months, thinks education is the key that will unlock many doors.

"All sides must see that times change and people change. If everyone learned this, many problems could be eliminated. My office not only works on the black-white problems but also with the young versus the old," Kroboth explained.

Each unit or squadron has an EOT representative, and if they can't solve the problem then Kroboth's office intercedes. He can go to the squadron commander of the base commander to help resolve the situation.

"About 75 per cent of the whites' problems are the 'lifer-first termer' type.

"The first termer can't be put down with, the 'That's the way its always been done' answers he receives from the senior NCOs. They seek the reason why, and I wholeheartly agree with them.

"For example, an E-4 came into my office and said 'I work six days a week and have to stay until closing time every day. My supervisor comes in at roll call, cuts out, doesn't come back until almost quitting time'. It is my job to eliminate this type of discrimination by talking to the supervisor and the man's squadron commander."

Kroboth also is one of four people at Osan that can place an off-base establishment off limits.

"This power makes the [illegible] ers [illegible] to me because they know it takes money [illegible] pocket when either the owners of the [illegible] refuse to [illegible]," Kroboth commented.

He said, "At one time there was a place outside the gates called '[illegible]' where only blacks would go. The whites would go to other bars. Now, anyone can visit any place and get served."

The EOT officer explained that trust plays a major role in his job. "The men, both black and white, must trust the man behind this job, in order to come here and not fear [illegible] cussions. I don't guarantee the problem can be eliminated overnight, but some positive [illegible] will happen, even if [illegible] ting all the [illegible] gether."

Kroboth put [illegible] saying, "I can [illegible] a man's [illegible] are something [illegible] crimination."

89

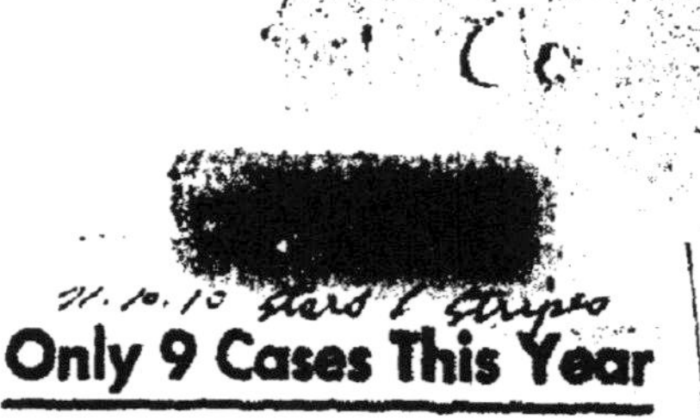

Only 9 Cases This Year

Airmen Aren't Using Osan Drug Program

By S. SGT. C. E. WITTER
S&S Staff Writer

OSAN AB—Hard drug users here who want help are getting it under the Air Force Limited Privileged Communication Program but marijuana users—and there are quite a few here according to one official—are not using the program.

Osan officials say that so far this year only nine men have turned themselves in, and that all of them were on hard drugs.

Capt. James Donat, assistant judge advocate, says the airmen feel marijuana is not harmful, so they don't turn themselves in.

Because Donat is a lawyer any conversations between him and a client are privileged communications, so many men come and talk to him about a variety of subjects, including drugs.

"To get into the LPC program, an airman must talk to either the base medical officer or his squadron commander. If he talks to me, he knows our talk is privileged communications. I can't say anything," Donat explained.

"However, if a pilot came to me and said he was using a hard drug, I would do my best, staying within the privileged communications bounds, to see to it that he was taken off flying status. This is to insure saving life and equipment," the lawyer said.

The lawyer's job in the Air Force drug campaign is to inform commanders on what action they can take against airmen, and to advise the troops of the program.

"At Osan we use a variety of methods of informing people about the LPC program. Lawyers and medical personnel speak at commanders call, special briefings, but by far the most popular way to get the message across is the informal rap sessions.

"These sessions reveal to me some of the reasons why the men turn to marijuana and other drugs, but mostly marijuana. They speak about group pressure, ease of getting the stuff and — most important — that no one has proved that grass is bad," Donat said.

"They just don't consider the stuff is harmful to them, because, for one, they still get their jobs done, and two, after work they want to unwind. And rather than go the way of the older enlisted man who drinks, the young ones smoke."

Getting the stuff at Osan is no problem. There are about 5,000 troops here, but very little trafficking of drugs on base, one official reported.

"You can get anything, from downers to pure "H", on just about any street corner outside the gates here," said Donat, "so why should anybody on base have to push it when they can go right off base and buy all they want?"

Local Korean police and military investigation officials know of this, but there is little they can do. One of reasons is because that pushers might be selling on one street one night and another one the next, police reported.

I spoke with 20 airmen, none over the grade of E5, asking if it was easy to get drugs off-base. Fourteen said they knew it was easy and could take me there and show me where to buy some. The rest said it was possible, they guessed, but couldn't be sure because they never tried.

A medical officer at Osan, Lt. Tom Adams, said there had been no deaths due to drugs here.

"If a man comes here to the hospital and is on drugs and wants help, we look after him. If the drug is a hard one, we send him to Tachikawa AB Hospital in Japan for treatment."

[illegible]

There to H[illegible] 시 ½

Stars & Stripes

Korean Police Join Military on Patrols

SUWON AB, Korea (Special) — Joint security patrols consisting of members of the Korean National Police (KNP) and the 6170th Combat Support Sq. security police are now in operation in Seryu Dong village.

About one month ago the security police section here put in a request to Yun Ki Won, then superintendent of the KNP, Suwon District, to allow a member of the KNP to accompany members of the security police on their nightly patrols of the local village.

The request was approved. Now a member of the KNP makes the nightly rounds with an interpreter and two security policemen from the security police section here.

Purpose of the patrols is to preserve order among members of the U.S. military and to give assistance and information. Due to the language barrier, the presence of the KNP has proven helpful.

"There have been a few minor incidents, but they have all been taken care of," stated M.Sgt. Pedro Villarreal, NCOIC of Law Enforcement and Air Base Defense. He added, "These patrols are at your service. They are not there as a threat. If anybody has any questions or problems, feel free to approach them."

91

4. 4차

1971. 11. 19.

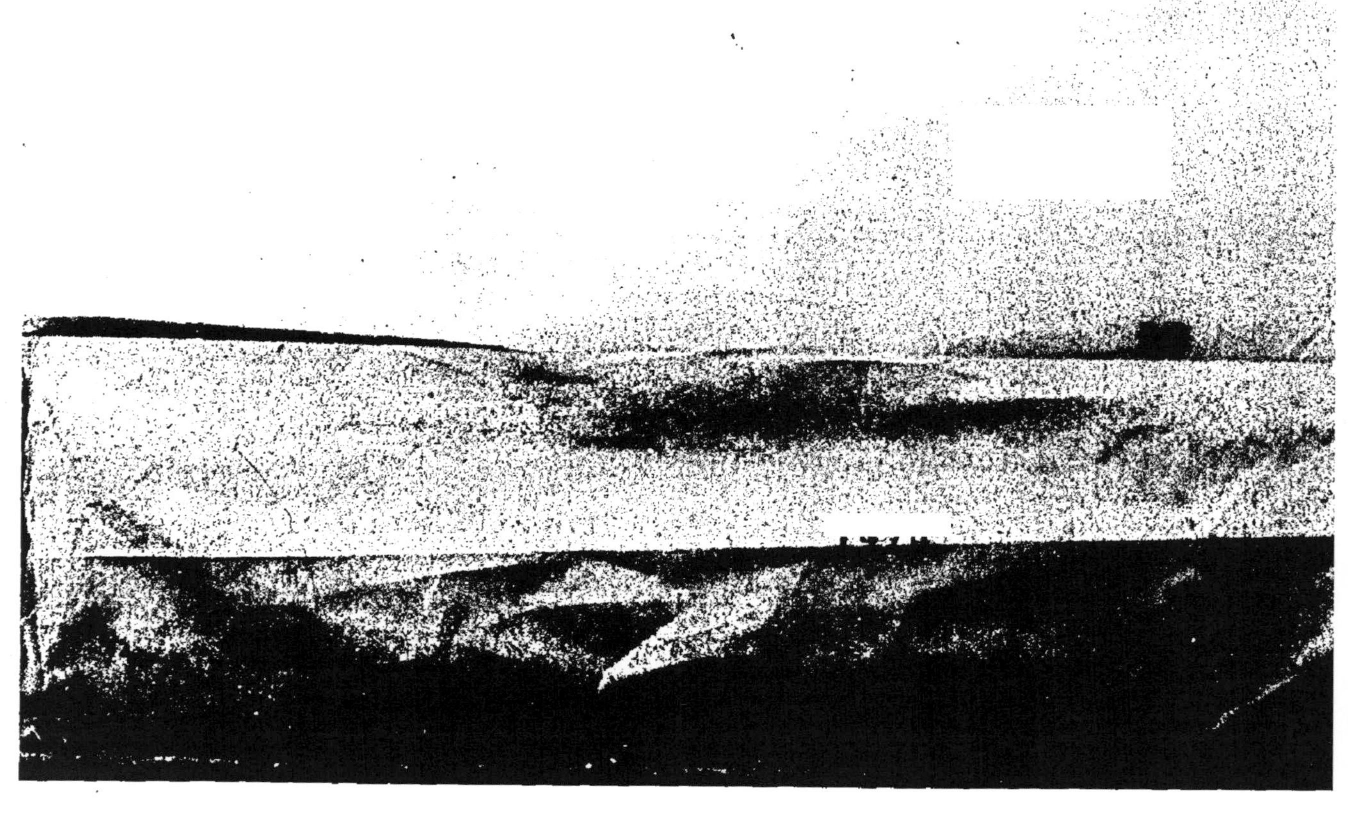

92

기 안 용 지

분류기호 문서번호	미이 723 -	(전화번호)	전결규정 조 항 국장 전결사항
처리기간			
시행일자	71. 10. 25.		
보존년한		국 장	
보조기관	북미 2과장		협조
기안책임자	권 찬	북미 2과 (71. 10. 25.)	
경유 수신 참조	SOFA 합동위 군,민관계 임시분과위원회 위원	발송 No. 2359 1971.10 25 외무부	통제
제목	이태원 기지촌 현지답사 계획 통보		

1. 한.미 합동 군,민관계 임시 분과위원회는 10. 28. 아래와 같은 세부 계획에 의거, 이태원 기지주변 현지답사 계획을 통보하오니 필히 참석하여 주시기 바랍니다.

- 아 래 -

17:50	미8군 Seoul Gerrison Command 정문앞 집합
18:00 - 19:00	의견 교환
19:15 - 20:15	Hartel House 에서 만찬
20:15 - 21:15	이태원 기지촌 현지답사

2. 제2차 보고서를 별첨하오니 참고하시기 바랍니다. 끝.

Panel 구성표

1. Panel on Local Community and Governmental Relations: (4)

   * 내무부 지방국 관리과장, 백세현 .... 22 - 2342 ①
   외무부 북미 2과, 김기조 .... 74 - 3073
   치안국 외사과, 이병모 .... 75 - 0951 ③
   교통부 진흥과장, 김철영 .... 75 - 4281 ③

2. Panel on Korean National Police-US Military Police Cooperation and Coordination: (3)

   * 치안국 외사과, 이병모 .... 72 - 1517
   외무부 북미 2과, 김기조 .... 74 - 3073
   치안국 수사 2계장 송형식 .... 75 - 0951 ④

3. Panel on Health and Sanitation: (3)

   * 보건사회부 보건관리관, 민창동 .... 75 - 6881 ⑤
   외무부 북미 2과, 권 찬 .... 74 - 3073
   교통부 관광국 업무과장, 김원효 .... 75 - 4281

4. Panel on Narcotics and Drug Control: (5)

   * 보건사회부 보건관리관, 민창동 .... 75 - 6881
   외무부 북미 2과, 권 찬 .... 74 - 3073
   치안국 수사 2계장, 송형식 .... 75 - 0951
   법무부 검찰과, 현홍주 .... 73 - 7625 ⑥
   법무부 송무과, 정구영 .... 72 - 7160 ⑦

94

5. Panel on Larceny and Black Marketing: (5)

*치안국 수사2계장, 송형식 .... 75 - 0951
외무부 북미2과, 권 찬 .... 74 - 3073
법무부 검찰과, 현홍주 .... 73 - 7625
법무부 총무과, 정구영 .... 72 - 7160
재무부 (관세청 대표) .... 72 - 0286

6. Panel on Race Relations and Equality of Treatment: (4)

*외무부 북미2과장, 김영섭 .... 74 - 3073
외무부 북미2과, 김기조 .... 74 - 3073
교통부 관광국 진흥과장, 김철영 .... 75 - 4281
문화공보부 해외과장, 최상학 .... 72 - 6121 ⑧

7. Panel on People-to-People Projects: (4)

*문화공보부 해외과장, 최상학 .... 72 - 6121
외무부 북미2과, 김기조 .... 74 - 3073
내무부 지방국 관리과장, 백세현 .... 22 - 2342
교통부 관광국 진흥과장, 김철영 .... 75 - 4281

95

STAFFING OF PANELS
AD HOC SUBCOMMITTEE-US COMPONENT

1. Panel on Local Community and Governmental Relations.

LTC Walter Kolditz, J5, Chairman (Y6046, 43-0283)
Mr. George Kim, G1; LCDR Robert E. Spydell, J1; MAJ Walter Ryland, PAJ, CPT James L. Donat, USAF; and Mr. J. A. McReynolds, J5.

2. Panel on Korean National Police-US Military Police Cooperation and Coordination.

MAJ J. J. Hallihan, PMJ, Chairman (Y6421)
LTC R. S. McCaul, G1; LCDR Robert E. Spydell, J1; LTC R. E. Fisher, USAF; and Mr. J. A. McReynolds, J5.

3. Panel on Health and Sanitation.

COL I. W. Daniele, Surgeon, Chairman (Y3161/6028)
CPT James G. Schwarz, USAF; Mr. T. J. Wash, ENJ; and Mr. J. A. McReynolds, J5.

4. Narcotics and Drug Control.

LTC W. E. Ray, J1, Chairman (Y3172/6040)
LTC Richard T. Brittain, G1; CPT James G. Schwarz; CPT M. J. Wentink, JAJ; MAJ Dick Petersen, J5; and Mr. W. D. Heaney, US Embassy.

5. Panel on Larceny and Black Marketing.

MAJ Charles A. Hines, PMJ, Chairman (Y6290)
COL D. F. McFall, Jr, J1; LTC R. S. McCaul, G1; LTC Ralph E. Fisher, USAF; CPT D. R. Dewall, JAJ; and Mr. Frank Cook, J5.

6. Panel on Race Relations and Equality of Treatment.

COL F. E. Norwalk, G1, Chairman (Y6960)
MAJ M. K. Wheeler, J1; Mr. Charles Farmer, CPO; CPT Thomas Kroboth, USAF; and Mr. Frank Cook, J5.

7. Panel on People-to-People Projects.

LTC R. S. McCaul, G1, Chairman (Y3175/6183, 42-0168)
COL D. F. McFall, Jr, J1; Mr. Benjamin B. Weems, PAJ; Mr. George Kim, G1; LTC M. W. Kohut, USAF, and Mr. Robert A. Kinney, J5.

96

The ROK Panels

		Tel:
1.	Panel on Local Community and Governmental Relations:	
	*PAIK Sae Hyun, Chief, Management Section, Local Administration Bureau, MOHA	22-2342
	KIM Kee Joe, North America Section II, MOFA	74-3073
	LEE Byung Mo, Senior Superintendent, National Police Bureau, MOHA	75-0951
	KIM Chul Yong, Chief, Promotion Section, Tourism Bureau, MOT	75-4281
2.	Panel on Korean National Police-US Military Police Cooperation and Coordination:	
	*LEE Byong Mo, Senior Superintendent, National Police Bureau, MOHA	75-0951
	KIM Kee Joe, North America Section II, MOFA	74-3073
	SONG Hyong Sik, Senior Superintendent, National Police, MOHA	75-0951
3.	Panel on Health and Sanitation:	
	*MIN Chang Dong, Public Health Officer, Public Health Bureau, MOH & SA	75-6881
	KWON Chan, North America Section II, MOFA	74-3073
	KIM Won Hyo, Chief, Business Section, Tourism Bureau, MOT	75-4281
4.	Panel on Narcotics and Drug Control:	
	*MIN Chang Dong, Public Health Officer, Public Health Bureau, MOH & SA	75-6881
	KWON Chan, North America Section II, MOFA	74-3073

91

SONG Hyong Sik, Senior Superintendent, National Police Bureau, MOHA — 75-0951

HYUN Hong Joo, Prosecution Section, Prosecution Bureau, MOJ — 73-7625

CHUNG Ku Young, Claims Section, Legal Affairs Bureau, MOJ — 72-7160

5. Panel on Larceny and Black Marketing:

*SONG Hyong Sik, Senior Superintendent, National Police Bureau, MOHA — 75-0951

KWON Chan, North America Section II, MOFA — 74-3073

HYUN Hong Joo, Prosecution Section, Prosecution Bureau, MOJ — 73-7625

CHUNG Ku Young, Claims Section, Legal Affairs Bureau, MOJ — 72-7160

Representative, Customs Bureau, MOF — 72-0286

6. Panel on Race Relations and Equality of Treatment:

*KIM Young Sup, Chief, North America Section II, MOFA — 74-3073

KIM Kee Joe, North America Section II, MOFA — 74-3073

KIM Chul Yong, Chief, Promotion Section, MOT — 75-4281

CHOI Sang Hak, Chief, Overseas Information Section, MOC & I — 72-6121

7. Panel on People-to-People Projects:

*CHOI Sang Hak, Chief, Overseas Information Section, MOC & I — 72-6121

KIM Kee Joe, North America Section II, MOFA — 74-3073

PAIK Sae Hyun, Chief, Management Section, Local Administration Bureau, MOHA — 22-2342

KIM Chul Yong, Chief, Promotion Section, Tourism Bureau, MOT — 75-4281

* denotes chairman.

98

공 란

공 

공 란

공 란

공 란

공 란

공 란

공　　란

공 

공 란

공 란

공 란

공 란

공 

공 란

공 란

공 란

공 란

공 란

공 란

공 란

공 란

공　　란

공

공 

공 란

공 란

공 란

공 란

공 란

공 란

공 란

공 란

공 란

공 란

공 란

공 란

공 란

공 란

공 

공 란

공 란

공 란

공 란

공 란

공 란

공 란

공 란

공

공 란

공 란

공 란

공 란

공 란

공 란

공　　　란

공 란

공 란

공 란

공 란

공 란

공 란

공 란

공　　　　란

공 란

공 란

공 란

공 란

공 란

SOF[illegible]ittee Meets

ROK, U.S. Agree To Fight Race Bias

SEOUL (Special) — The ROK-U.S. Status of Forces Agreement (SOFA) Joint Committee received the fourth report of its Ad Hoc subcommittee on civil-military relations and approved five recommendations submitted by the subcommittee at its 69th meeting held in U.S. SOFA conference room Thursday.

These recommendations include one from the panel on larceny and black marketing and four on race relations and equal treatment.

The five approved recommendations, coupled with nine recommendations approved by the Joint Committee last month, are part of a continuing effort designed to improve civil and military relations between the Korean people and U.S. servicemen.

The approved recommendations provide for closer ROK-U.S. mutual cooperation in dealing with larceny and black marketing, as well as joint U.S.-ROK efforts to eliminate inequality of treatment toward both American and Korean personnel in camp communities.

[illegible] Committee also approved a recommendation of its transportation subcommittee relating to a change in procedures in licensing and registration of privately-owned vehicles of USFK personnel and U.S. invited contractor personnel in connection with a reregistration and licensing of all such vehicles during January 1972.

[illegible] ROK-U.S. [illegible] Committee also approved nine recommendations by the facilities and areas subcommittee and assigned three new tasks to that subcommittee. The U.S. representative, Lt. Gen. Robert N. Smith, presided at this meeting, which was the last for Koo Choong Whay, the ROK representative. He is being reassigned as minister of the ROK Mission at the United Nations in New York City.

The next meeting of the SOFA Joint Committee is scheduled for Jan. 27 in the ROK Capitol Building.

168

'Tact at All Times'

Stars & Stripes 71. 11. 19.

Courtesy Is Byword of Bar-Hopping Patrol

Sgt. 1.C. Hollis Schubert (left) and Sgt. 1.C. Norman Reeves

By GUNNERY SGT. JIM PAYNTER
S&S Korea Bureau

SEOUL — Schubert and Reeves went bar-hopping the other night, and they did it while on duty.

Bert and Harry will be doing the same thing: wandering from bar to bar while on duty.

The bar-hopping is part of a new program for the Yongsan area called the "Courtesy Patrol," which sends two E7s or E8s out every night into Itaewon, the local bar district, on a roving patrol.

During the daytime, two senior NCOs visit wherever a crowd is likely to gather, the Service Club, bus stops and exchanges, as they patrol the base. At night, two men patrol the local bar district and two more patrol the post.

Their job is to render assistance and enforce required standards of dress, appearance and conduct" among the soldiers off duty.

And, according to Sgt. Maj. William J. Sweeney, Yongsan Garrison Command Sergeant Major, they must do it in a way "befitting both a senior NCO — which is the patrol — and the soldier involved."

To paraphrase the sergeant major, the old "brown shoe army" approach to correcting a soldier while on courtesy patrol is out; the modern Army approach of respect for human rights and feelings is the way it is to be done.

In fact, the third order on the instruction sheet for the Courtesy Patrol is "use common sense, courtesy and tact at all times."

"Of course," said Sweeney, "if these senior NCOs encounter resistance, they aren't going to back away from it. They are, after all, senior NCOs."

In the case of resistance to the suggestion that a soldier tuck in his shirt or head back to the post before he becomes too drunk to take care of himself, the Courtesy Patrol can either write a report on the incident or call in the military police.

"The patrol shows that we're thinking of the soldier's welfare," said Sweeney. "If he dresses in a fashion repulsive to the Koreans, we're doing him a favor by monitoring him."

Not all of the those on patrol agree with the sergeant major, however.

"It's a waste of time," said Sgt. 1.C. Hollis R. Schubert. "The Ps (military policemen) don't help me with my job, why should I help them with theirs?

Schubert's partner for the night, Sgt. 1.C. Norman Reeves, generally agreed with Schubert. "When somebody is going to fight, there is nothing we can do about it. That's a job for the MPs, not us."

When asked if the young soldier who is to asked to tuck in his shirt might think he is being harassed by a "lifer," Reeves said, "you're damn right. When they get off post, they've had enough of being told what to do all day. They don't want to see me out here, at least not in uniform."

First Sgt. Ben Roberts, who has been in the Army 28 years if you include four years of reserve duty, says it's just another extra duty.

"I've pulled duties like this before," Roberts said, "we've always had courtesy patrols in the Army. This is just the first one I've had that we wore uniforms and brassards."

Does the patrol do any good? "Why sure it does," said Roberts. "When someone is wearing a field jacket with civilian clothes — which is against 8th Army regulations — they have to be told about it. When something is wrong, when a regulation is broken, it has to be corrected."

"But," said his partner, Sgt. 1.C. Donald C. Fleming, "if the junior NCOs, the corporals and sergeants, were doing their job, we wouldn't have to be out here. If the platoon sergeant and section chiefs were doing their job like they used to, the men would know that they must obey the regs."

"Yeah", agreed Roberts, "but they don't, and something has to be done, so here we are. It's just another extra duty, like I said before."

Schubert and Reeves also mentioned that the military policemen in the ASCOM area had asked that the patrol be discontinued.

But, according to one of the military policemen patrolling the Itaewon area, "they save us a lot of work. If we see someone too drunk to take care of himself, we take him back to the post. A lot of time he doesn't exactly want to go, or thinks he's not as drunk as we think he is, and it ends up as an arrest."

"Damn right I'd rather talk to the Courtesy Patrol than get hauled in by the Ps," said a beer-drinking soldier. "If the P's see you out of uniform, they run you in. They're all young and their power has gone to their heads. But if the Courtesy Patrol sees you doing something wrong, they just tell you about it. As long as you don't give them any trouble, that's as far as it goes."

In the meantime, Schubert and Reeves prowl the streets and bars of Itaewon about once every 20 days, using, according to their orders, "common sense, courtesy and tact at all times."

169

[illegible] — the American soldier has been found guilty by a Seoul court of bringing 17 television sets into Korea illegally, Korean authorities said Wednesday.

Spec. 5 Richard N. Trabert was sentenced Nov. 12 to confinement at hard labor for one year, and was assessed 1.75 million won (about $3,800) for sending the television sets to Korea from Japan via the Army Post Office.

The prison sentence was suspended for two years, Korean officials said, and the assessment may be collected only by civil suit of the customs authorities against Trabert.

Trabert was apprehended by Korean authorities July 23. He is assigned to Headquarters, 8th Army, they said.

both in money and other incentives, such as early DEROS and passes.

Monetary rewards can be of up to $100 cash, depending on the size and significance of the arrest. The monetary reward portion of the new program has already been put into effect, and cash rewards will be paid to informants by 8th Army Hq. based on recommendations from the 7th MP Group (CL).

KORSCOM sub-area commanders are now in the process of establishing local policy for other awards — deciding what they will be and how they will be granted. Awards suggested by 8th Army and KORSCOM Hq. include up to 30-day drops in DEROS dates, reassignment within Korea, letters of commendation and passes.

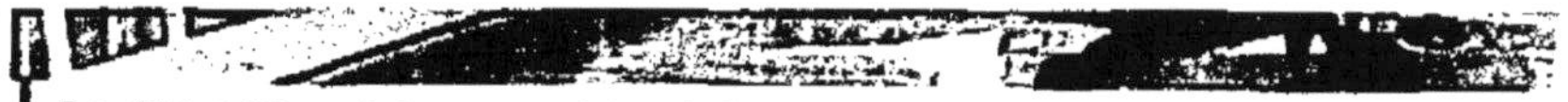

Sgt. Maj. William J. Sweeney points out the correct Army haircut policy that the Courtesy Patrol looks for on their nightly rounds of Yongsan and Itaewon.

170

Congressional Hearing

Black GIs Talking Revolt: Prober

Compiled From UPI and AP

WASHINGTON—A report to a congressional hearing on military racial policies said Wednesday black servicemen "are already talking in terms of revolution and some type of violence is inevitable."

Thaddeus Garrett Jr., assistant to Rep. Shirley Chisholm, D-N.Y., co-chairman of the hearing with Rep. Ronald V. Dellums, D-Calif., said he drafted the report after a six-week tour of U.S. military bases abroad.

"The feeling among blacks stationed in Europe is that military standards apply in different degrees to whites than to themselves," Garrett said in the report as Negro lawmakers known as the Black Caucus opened the second day of their unofficial hearings.

Dellums marked the start of the sessions Tuesday with release of what he called secret Pentagon papers allegedly showing an agreement between the State Department and the government of Iceland against stationing blacks in that country.

The documents, all marked "confidential" and "secret," consisted of three memos exchanged between State Department and Navy officials. Dellums said they were mailed to him anonymously and he added he was told that similar agreements had been made with West Germany, Greece and Turkey, but that he did not have documents to back up that report at this time.

One memo, dating back to 1961, quoted then U.S. Ambassador to Iceland James K. Penfield as stating that the "Icelandic government will have no objections to 'three or four' colored servicemen in the defense force but hope that they will be carefully chosen in light of the special conditions existing in Iceland."

Another memo, circulated within the Navy Department, declared that "although nothing has been put in writing, it has been anonymously expressed by various members of the government of Iceland that black servicemen are not desired in Iceland. Further, it was indicated that this statement would be denied if questioned, was to be unofficial and attributable to no specific person."

Garrett said he feared "after many discussions with those who sit in the seats of command, that the explosiveness which prevails is made more serious by the amazing fact that many of those in command positions on all levels refuse to realize that even in a relatively controlled society as the military, racism was and does exist.

"One black soldier at the Mannheim (Germany) compound, Pfc. Donald Barber, reported that blacks there are already talking in terms of revolution and that some type of violence is inevitable, that they just do not care anymore," Garrett said.

The main problem areas, he said, are those of military justice in which a disproportionate number of blacks are jailed, denied adequate legal defense, and are beaten. Other areas are in promotions and job placements within the military.

The general consensus among young blacks is that "the potential for violence is quite real," Garrett concluded.

In other cases cited at the hearing:

An American black soldier said he was hosed down and left lying in the water for two days in a stockade as punishment at a U.S. Army base overseas.

A nightclub in Frankfurt, Germany, tries to exclude Negroes by putting up a "Members Only" sign, said a black military man who once was refused entrance.

And blacks at Minot Air Force Base, N.D., complained that "roving patrols" seek out men who don't wear their hair in acceptable military fashion.

172 , 173 페이지오류

172, 173 페이지오류

軍·民関係 臨時 分科委員会

活動 報告 및 対策

1972. 1. 7.

外務部 欧美局

軍民関係臨時分科委員会活動報告 및 対策

1. 設置目的 및 経緯

1971.7.9. 平沢에서 発生한 黒人兵士와 現地住民들간의 衝突事件은 黒人에 対한 韓国人의 人種差別이 原因인듯이 外信에 報道되어 美国에서 物議를 이르켰고, Dellums 의원을 為始한 一部 黒人議員들은 韓国人의 黒人差別待遇를 猛烈히 非難하고 韓国에 対한 美国의 援助中断을 主張하기에 이르렀음.

外務部는 駐美 各公館에 訓令하여 当該議員 및 主要言論機関을 相対로 実情을 알리고 解明하도록 指示하는 한편, 韓・美合同委員会를 通하여 美側과 対策을 協議하였으며 問題의 深刻性에 비추어 그 根本的 解決을 為하여는 基地周辺에서 뿐만 아니라 中央에서도 韓・美間의 緊密한 協力이 必要하며 또한 政府関係部処의 共同努力이 必須的임을 判断하고 8.30. 外務部長官이 国務会議에 韓・美合同委員会傘下에 새로운 分科委員会設置를 計劃하고 있음을 報告하였음. 다음날 8.31. 駐韓美大使는 外務部長官을 訪問하고 「닉슨」大統領이 国務, 国防 両長官에게 示達한 指示覚書와 또 両長官이 美軍駐屯 各国에 人種差別을 除去하기 為해 指示한 示達書를 提示하고 우리側의 協力을 要請하였음.

外務部長官은 이에 積極 協調할것을 約束하였으며 韓・美合同委員会에서 이 問題 解決을 為한 分委를 構成할 予定임을 알리고 美側의 協調도 당부하였음. 그後 9.2. 韓・美合同委員会는 그의 実務機関으로서 軍民関係臨時分科委員会 (The Ad Hoc Subcommittee on Civil-Military Relations)를 緊急課題로서 設置하였고 (構成表別紙) 同分科委員会傘下에 韓・美実務者로 構成되는 아래의 7個 調査班 (PANEL)을 構成하였음.

-1-

195

分科委員構成

韓國側			美國側
議長	金泳燮	外務部北美2課長	Captain Frank M. Romaniok, J5
幹事	金基光	外務部北美2課書記官	Mr. Robert A. Kinney, J5
委員	白世鉉	內務部管理課長	Colonel David P. Heekin, USA
	宋亨植	治安局搜査2係長	Colonel Robert G. Eklund, USAF
	李丙禎	治安局外事3係長	Colonel Bruce T. Coggins, USA
	[illegible]	法務部訟務課檢事	Colonel James K. Pope, USA
	玄尙柱	法務部檢察課檢事	Colonel Robert J. Kriwanek, USA
	金徹濟	交通部振興課長	Mr. John P. Leonard, American Embassy
	[illegible]	保健社會部保健行政官	
	[illegible]	文公部海外課長	

Panel 構成表

1. Panel on Local Community and Governmental Relations: (10명)

※白世鉉 內務部管理課長	※ LTC Walter Kolditz, J5
金基光 外務部北美2課	Mr. George Kim, G1
李丙禎 治安局外事課	LCDR Robert E. Spydell, J1
金徹濟 交通部振興課長	MAJ Walter Ryland, PAJ
	CPT James L. Donat, USAF
	Mr. J. A. Moreynolds, J5

176

2. Panel on Korean National Police - US Military Police Cooperation and Coordination: (8명)

* 李丙模 治安局 外事課	* MAJ J. J. Hallihan, PMJ
金基光 外務部 北美2課	LTC R. S. McCaul, G1
宋字植 治安局 捜査2係長	LCDR Robert E. Spydell, J1
	LTC R. E. Fisher, USAF
	Mr. J. A. Moreynolds, J5

3. Panel on Health and Sanitation: (7명)

* 閔和東 保健社会部 保健管理官	* COL I. W. Daniels, Surgeon
柳 燦 外務部 北美2課	CPT James G. Schwars, USAF
金琢淳 交通部 業務課長	Mr. T. J. Wash, EAEM
	Mr. J. A. Moreynolds, J5

4. Panel on Narcotics and Drug Control: (13명)

* 閔和東 保健社会部 保健管理官	* LTC W. E. Ray, J1
柳 燦 外務部 北美2課	COL W. R. Warren, Surgeon
宋字植 治安局 捜査2係長	LTC Richard T. Brittain, G1
文炳柱 法務部 検察課, 検事	CPT James G. Schwars, USAF
鄭鉉永 法務部 法務課, 検事	CPT M. J. Wentink, JAJ
	MAJ Dick Petersen, J5
	CW2 Jesse C. Magee, PMJ
	Mr. W. D. Ebaney, US Embassy

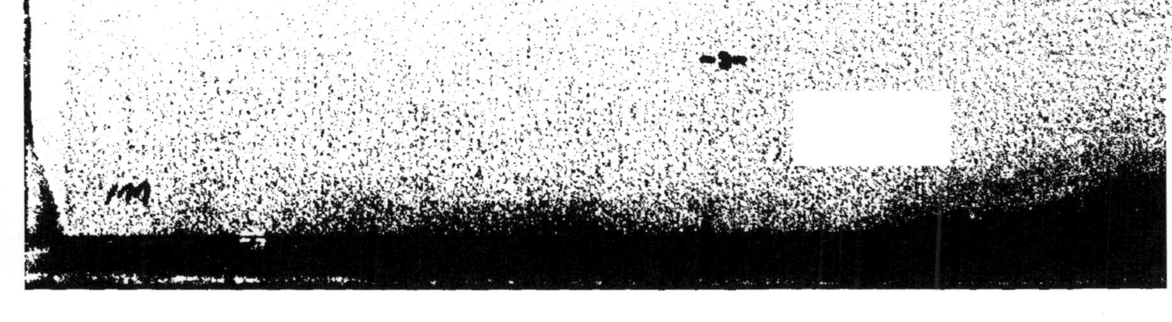

5. Panel on Larceny and Black Marketing: (11명)

※ 宋 孝 植	治安局 捜査2係長	※ MAJ Charles A. Hines, PMJ
朴 　 煥	外務部 北美2課	COL D. F. McFall, Jr, J1
文 鴻 柱	法務部 検察課, 検事	LTC R. S. McCaul, G1
鄭 緑 永	法務部 訟務課, 検事	LTC Ralph E. Fisher, USAF
申 水 洙	関税庁 心理課長	CPT D. R. Decaul, JAJ
		Mr. Frank Cook, J5

6. Panel on Race Relations and Equality of Treatment: (10명)

※ 金 泳 燮	外務部 北美2課長	※ COL F. E. Norwalk, G1
金 基 兆	外務部 北美2課	MAJ M. K. Wheeler, J1
金 徹 淳	交通部 監理課長	Mr. Charles Farmer, CPO
崔 相 学	文化公報部 海外課長	CPT Thomas Kroboth, USAF
		CPT Larry L. Raab, PMJ
		Mr. Frank Cook, J5

7. Panel on People-to-People Projects: (10명)

※ 崔 相 学	文化公報部 海外課長	※ LTC R. S. McCaul, G1
金 基 兆	外務部 北美2課	COL D. F. McFall, Jr, J1
白 世 鉉	内務部 管理課長	Mr. Benjamin B. Weems, PAJ
金 徹 淳	交通部 監理課長	Mr. George Kim, G1
		LTC M. W. Kohut, USAF
		Mr. Robert A. Kinney, J5

2. 分科委活動 經緯

가. 会議經過

(1) 第1次会議開催(9.7.)

駐韓 美軍들과 基地村 住民들과의 問題点을 調査하기 위하여 두개 基地村 一帶에 情報蒐集 調査를 實施키로 결의함. (東豆川, 안정리) —合同委 報告,通過되었음. (65次)

(2) 第2次会議 開催(9.22)

5個 基地村 地域에 情報蒐集 調査를 實施키로 合意함. (오산, 大邱, Ascom, 群山, 梨泰院)—合同委 報告, 通過되었음. (66 次)

(3) 第3次会議 開催(10.18.)

7個 調査班(Panel)을 構成하기로 合意하고 各調査班에 委員들을 위촉함. 또 調査班의 活動 限界와 節次 問題를 討議함.—合同委 報告, 通過되었음. (67次)

(4) 第4次会議 開催(11.19.)

5個 調査班의 報告書 및 建議事項(Recommendations)을 접수하고 通過시킴.—合同委 報告,通過되었음. (68次)

(5) 第5次会議 開催(12.14)

2個 調査班의 建議事項을 접수하고 通過시킴.—合同委 報告,通過되었음. (69次)

(6) 第6次会議 開催

外務部 会議室에서 1.24. 14:00에 開催 豫定

나. 情報蒐集 現地踏査 活動

	日時	地域	美軍基地
(1)	9.10.	東豆川	Camp Casey
(2)	9.13.	平澤	Camp Humphreys
(3)	9.24.	平澤	Osan Air Base
(4)	9.28.	大邱	Camp Walker, Henry
(5)	9.30.	富平	Ascom
(6)	10. 7.	群山	Kunsan Air Base
(7)	10.28.	梨泰院	Seoul Garrison Command
(8)	11.15.	釜山	Hialeah Compound
(9)	11.30.	坡州郡	Camp Rice
(10)	12. 3.	大田	Camp Ames

180

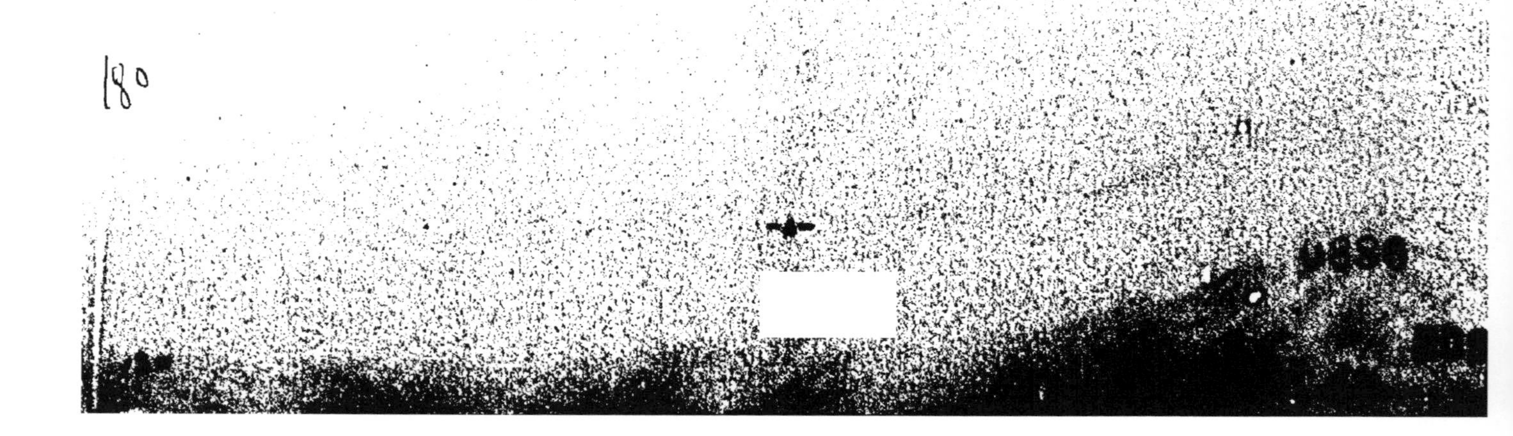

3. 臨時分科委員会가 採択한 韓美 両国 対政府 建議事項(Recommendations)

가. 地方行政関係

建議題目 : 地域関係 諮問委員会 (The Community Relations Advisory Councils)의 名称 改正

内 容 : (1) 韓国 政府와 駐韓美軍 当局은 地域関係 諮問委員会를 韓美親善協議会 (The Korean American Friendship Councils)로 名称을 改正할것.

(2) 韓·美 両側 共히 適正한 「레벨」에서 韓·美親善協議会를 組織할것.

나. 韓国 警察 및 美 憲兵間의 協調問題

1) 建議題目 : 韓·美 合同軍警巡察班 設置

内 容 : 設置 可能한 場所에는 어느 地域에나 韓·美 合同軍警巡察班을 設置할것.

2) 建議題目 : 韓·美 合同軍警巡察班의 協調増進

内 容 : 韓国 警察当局 및 駐韓 美軍憲兵司令部는 警察情報의 交換, 合同巡察活動의 強化 및 相互 問題点을 討議하기 위하여 定期的인 Channel을 設定하여 運営할것.

다. 保健·衛生問題

1) 建議題目 : 性病의 原因 除去

内 容 : 性病 予防을 担当하는 韓·美 関係当局은 性病保有者로 하여금 治療토록 하고 完治될 때까지 公衆으로부터 隔離토록 할것. 韓国 関係当局과 美軍 当局은 性病의 原因除去 및 予防에 関한 教育,計劃을 함께 세우도록 할것.

2) 建議題目 : 韓国 「크럽」 便所施設의 衛生 改善

-7-

181

內　　容：韓國 保健當局은 美軍當局의 協調를 얻어 基地村 韓國「크럽」所有者에게 다음과 같은 緊急措置를 取하도록 할것.

(1) 便所의 洗滌물이 適切히 나오도록 함.

(2) 수건, 종이 등을 備置토록 함.

(3) 便器 洗滌, 消毒, 종이나 수건 등을 提供하는 사람을 配置토록 함.

라. 痲藥問題

協議題目：痲藥 取締管理에 대한 責任

內　　容：韓·美 關係當局이 協調하여 共同으로 다음 特定分野에 대한 一次的 責任을 짐. 韓國 關係當局은 韓國에서 生産되거나 韓國에 違法 輸入된 痲藥管理를 責任지며, 美國 當局은 美軍에 依한 痲藥 不法輸入 및 美軍 相互間 痲藥取引을 管理하는 責任을 짐.

마. 盜難 및 闇市場 問題

協議題目：美 政府 所有軍需品의 盜難 및 免稅軍需品의 不正處理로 因한 國庫損失防止策

內　　容：(1) 駐韓 美軍의 效果的인 作戰에 障害를 가져올 程度로 美國 政府 所有軍需品의 盜難이 頻繁함에 비추어서 大韓民國 政府의 關係機關 및 駐韓 美軍의 執行機關이 韓美 相互協力의 既存節次에 따라서 盜難된 美 政府 所有軍需品의 所有 및 運用을 禁止하도록 할것.

(2) 免稅軍需品의 不正處理가 韓國 經濟에 惡影響을 끼치고 韓國의 外貨收入에 큰 損失을 가져옴에 비추어 既存 韓·美 合同調査「팀」의 活動을 더욱 强化하고 擴大할것.

-6-

182

바. 人種差別問題

1) 建議題目: 美軍基地村 所在 韓國 遊興業體에서의 人種差別 撤廢

內　　容: 韓國 地方關係機關은 美軍基地 關係官과 協力하여 韓國 遊興業體에서 人種差別없이 待遇하도록 奬勵할것. 韓國 關係機關은 俸給날 및 週末 등과 같이 多數의 顧客이 올것이 予想되는 時期에는 顧客數에 알맞는 從業員을 配置토록 할것.

2) 建議題目: 美軍基地村 所在 遊興業體에서 雇傭하는 接待婦에 의한 人種差別 撤廢

內　　容: 韓國 地方關係 機關은 美軍基地 代表者와 協力하여 遊興業體에서 雇傭하는 接待婦가 顧客을 接待함에 있어서 差別待遇를 하지 않도록 奬勵할것. 美國 關係當局은 黑人 兵士들을 接待하는 業者의 接待婦를 差別하는 일이 없도록 白人 兵士들을 可能한 手段을 다하여 敎育하고 指導할것.

3) 建議題目: 基地村 所在 遊興業體에서 音樂 曲目 選択에 関한 差別 撤廢

內　　容: 韓國 地方關係機關은 美軍基地 代表者와 協力하여 遊興業體의 曲目選択에 있어서 顧客들의 嗜好에 따라 均衡있게 選択하도록 할것. 韓國 觀光協会와 美國 關係當局은 協力하여 遊興業體가 広範한 種類의 「레코드」를 갖게하고 出演 樂士들이 여러 種類의 曲目을 演奏할 수 있도록 訓練하도록 할것.

4) 建議題目: 基地村 周辺에서의 韓·美 軍警察間의 協調増進

內　　容: 基地村 地域의 韓國 警察과 美 憲兵은 韓·美 軍警察 當局間의 友好増進을 위해 最善을 다할것.

-7-

183

사. 対民関係

1) 建議題目 : 「헬로 코리아」 TV「프로그램」의 促進

內　　容 : 美軍의 韓国 理解에 도움을 주는 「헬로 코리아」TV「프로그램」의 重要性을 認識하며 韓·美 当局은 必要한 財政的 支援을 優先的으로 하며, 特히 僻地 美軍들에게 同「프로」를 볼 수 있도록 할것.

2) 建議題目 : 韓·美 文化에 対한 가용자의 製作 및 普及

內　　容 : 美軍이 韓国文化를 알고 韓国民이 美国文化를 알 수 있도록 韓国 政府와 美軍 当局은 文化資料準備를 위한 予算措置를 할것. 또 同 資料는 巡回하면서 使用할 수 있는 「스라이드」, 映画 등 紹介資料를 包含하여야 하고 韓·美 両国民의 知識과 理解를 増進하기 위한 韓·美文化의 여러가지 面을 紹介토록 考案되어야 함.

外務部는 上記 対政府 建議案이 回信에 依하여 合意 採択됨에 따라 이를 関係 各 部処에 通告하여 그 施行에 万全을 期하도록 措置하였음.

4. 外務部는 앞으로 臨時分科委員會에 다음 對策方案을 提示하고 美側의 이에 對한 協助를 要請할 方針임.

가. 性病豫防 및 治療對策

(1) 美國軍 當局에게 美軍 營內에 出入하는 職業女性(例: 동두천에는 1日에 4-500名에 達함)이 등록증과 檢診證을 提示케 한 後 通過시키도록 要求한다. (外務部, 交通部, 保社部, 治安局)

(2) 職業女性中 未登錄 女性의 美軍人 接待를 根絶시킨다.

(가) 美側은 美 兵士에게 登錄證과 檢診證을 確認토록 敎育시킨다 (外務部)

(나) 韓國 警察은 未登錄 女性의 營業行爲를 적발 의법 응징한다. (交通部 治安局, 保社部)

나. 麻藥 및 習慣性醫藥品의 團束

(1) 麻藥 및 習慣性醫藥品의 APO를 通한 반입을 防止하기 爲하여 現在 10%로 되어있는 小包檢査 制度와는 關係없이 科學的 方法, 警察犬等을 利用하여 韓·美 合同으로 적발한다. (外務部, 財務部, 保社部, 治安局, 法務部)

(2) 麻藥 및 習慣性 醫藥品 常習 使用者 團束

(가) 美 當局은 常習 軍人의 外出을 禁한다. (外務部)

(나) 韓國 當局은 常習 職業女性의 登錄을 박탈한다. 登錄 박탈자의 他地方 轉出을 不可能케 한다. (交通部, 保社部, 治安局)

다. 軍需品 盜難 및 闇去來 防止

(1) 軍需品을 절취하여 韓國人에게 販賣하는 美軍人을 적발, 의법 處罰하는 措置를 強化하도록 美側에 要求한다. (外務部, 治安局, 財務部)

(2) 廢棄 處分된 軍需 物品을 再生한것은 盜難品으로 간주하지 않도록 一定한 한계를 美側과 協議 設定한다. (外務部, 治安局, 財務部)

(3) 美軍 兵士의 外出時 携帶許容品(例: 洋酒 1상자등)을 縮小 制限하도록 美側에 要求한다. (外務部, 治安局, 財務部)

라. 軍票의 不法去來

(1) 軍票의 不法去來를 根絶하는 捷徑은 美軍 軍票(韓國과 越南에만 있음)의 韓國에서의 廢止인바, 이를 爲한 對美交涉을 재개(1968年에 始作함)한다. 이 交涉에 앞서 韓國에서 美 弗貨를 자유대한 通貨로 許容하도록 외환관리법을 改正한다. (外務部, 財務部)

(2) 上記가 관철될때까지 短期措置로 美 當局에게 軍票 交換所의 增設과 交換의 便利를 도모케하도록 要請한다. (外務部)

(가) 軍當門에 交換所를 상설한다.

(나) 觀光業所 集中地帶 인근에 交換所를 상설한다. (財務部, 交通部 協助 必要)

<<參考資料>>

(1) 美軍 犯罪事件 統計表(70-71)

(2) 駐韓美軍人 外出人員數

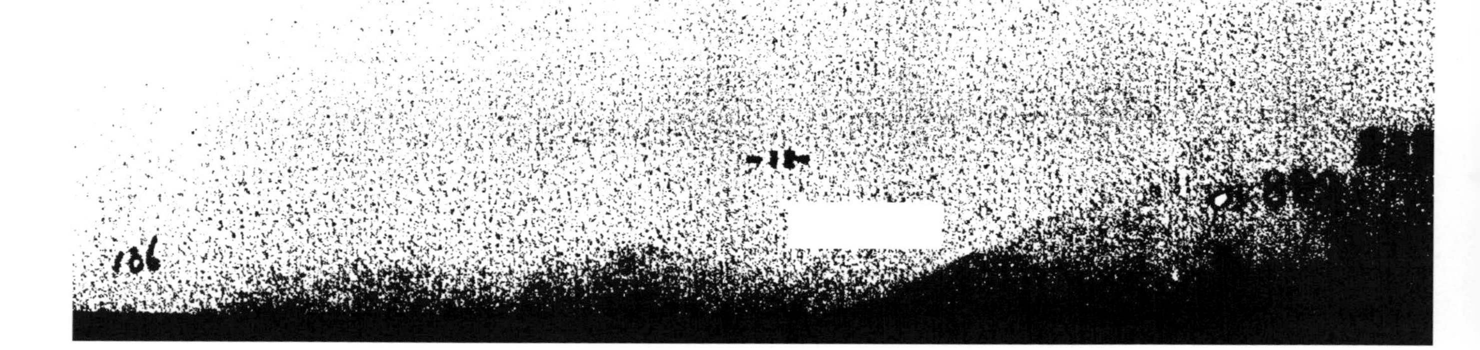

駐韓美軍人關聯事件統計表

(1970-71)

月數 ＼ 年數	70 年	71 年
1 月	40 件	46 件
2 月	44 件	29 件
3 月	52 件	56 件
4 月	56 件	33 件
5 月	53 件	30 件
6 月	42 件	273 件
7 月	35 件	100 件
8 月	41 件	109 件
9 月	18 件	113 件
10 月	33 件	101 件
11 月	37 件	113 件
12 月	27 件	
計	488 件	792 件

-13-

137

駐韓美軍人外出人員數

基地村名	美軍基地名	外出美軍人數(日平均)
梨泰院	USAGY	500
東豆川	Camp Casey	1,000
平澤郡 安井里	Camp Hovey Camp Humphreys	200
富平/新村	ASCOM	450
大田-장동리	Camp Ames	150
坡州郡 영주골	Camp Rice	150
大邱	Camp Henry Camp Walker	500
釜山	Hialeah Compound	400
春川	Camp page	200
原州	Camp Long	200
平澤郡 松炭邑	Osan AB	1,000
群山 Kunsan, Silvertown	Kunsan AB	500
[illegible]	Camp Carroll	300
光州(松汀)	Kwangju AB	200
馬山	-	100
計		6,000

128

공 란

공 란

공 

공 란

공 란

공 란

공　　란

공　　　란

공 란

공 란

공 란

공 란

공 란

공 란

공 란

공

공 란

공　　란

공 

공 란

공 란

공　　　　란

공 란

공

공 란

외교문서 비밀해제: 주한미군지위협정(SOFA) 36

주한미군지위협정(SOFA) 군민관계 임시분과위원회 1

초판인쇄 2024년 03월 15일
초판발행 2024년 03월 15일

지은이 한국학술정보(주)
펴낸이 채종준
펴낸곳 한국학술정보(주)
주 소 경기도 파주시 회동길 230(문발동)
전 화 031-908-3181(대표)
팩 스 031-908-3189
홈페이지 http://ebook.kstudy.com
E-mail 출판사업부 publish@kstudy.com
등 록 제일산-115호(2000. 6. 19)

ISBN 979-11-7217-047-9 94340
979-11-7217-011-0 94340 (set)

책에 대한 더 나은 생각, 끊임없는 고민, 독자를 생각하는 마음으로 보다 좋은 책을 만들어갑니다.